ACHIEVING, BELIEVING, AND CARING

Dedication

Who Is to Blame?

The college professor said, "Such rawness in a student is a shame.
Lack of preparation in the high school is to blame."
Said the high school teacher:
"Good heavens! That boy's a fool.
The fault, of course, is with the middle school."
The middle school teacher said,
"From such stupidity may I be spared.
They sent him up so unprepared."
The primary teacher huffed, "Kindergarten blockheads all.
They call that preparation — Why, it's worse than none at all."
The Kindergarten teacher said, "Such lack of training never did I see.
What kind of a woman must that mother be?"
The mother said, "Poor helpless child — he's not to blame.
His father's people were all the same."
Said the father at the end of the line:
"I doubt the rascal's even mine!"

We live in a blaming society. Rarely do we ask "Why?" Instead, we almost always ask "Who?" Schools that show care have leaders that *continually* ask why and rarely ask who.

Teaching and learning staff are well aware of the media's willingness to heap blame on the public schools for society's ailments. These staff members desperately need leaders who do not all blame, but work with them to improve the system.

This book is dedicated to those leaders who are.

ACHIEVING
BELIEVING
AND CARING

Doing whatever it takes to create successful schools

CHRISTOPHER M. SPENCE

Pembroke Publishers Limited

To my wife, Marcia Monique Spence

© 2009 Pembroke Publishers
538 Hood Road
Markham, Ontario, Canada L3R 3K9
www.pembrokepublishers.com

Distributed in the U.S. by Stenhouse Publishers
480 Congress Street
Portland, ME 04101
www.stenhouse.com

We acknowledge the financial support of the Government of Canada through the Book Publishing Industry Development Program (BPIDP) for our publishing activities.

We acknowledge the assistance of the Government of Ontario through the Ontario Media Development Corporation's Ontario Book Initiative.

Library and Archives Canada Cataloguing in Publication

Spence, Christopher Michael

   Achieving, believing and caring : doing whatever it takes to create successful schools / Christopher M. Spence.

Includes index.
ISBN 978-1-55138-248-7

   1. Educational leadership. 2. School management and organization. I. Title.

LB2805.S634 2009   371.2   C2009-902719-4

Editor: Kate Revington
Cover Design: John Zehethofer
Typesetting: Jay Tee Graphics Ltd.

Printed and bound in Canada
9 8 7 6 5 4 3 2 1

Contents

Foreword

Dr. Chris Spence's insight into our educational system and its potential both to shape the academic and intellectual well-being of our youths and to create socially stable and law-abiding communities is profound and innovative. In *Achieving, Believing, and Caring*, Spence exhibits a deep understanding of the complex causes of the social and emotional unrest that leads many young people into situations where they are in conflict with the law, be it as perpetrators of violence, as members of gangs, or as victims of youth crime. He argues that, if we as a society truly care about the today and tomorrow of our children, we need to develop schools that care.

Spence sees our public schools as "microcosms, the mirror and the heart and soul of our society." He feels that those who work in them need to create schools where all children, regardless of their backgrounds, parents' income, or parents' level of education, have the opportunity for a quality education. Emphasizing the need for schools to offer a nurturing environment, he believes that showing kindness to a student provides that student with hope, connects him or her with teachers and staff, and presents a model of proper behavior. With a connection between student and teachers, a rapport will evolve, and meaningful learning can take place.

Schools "cannot ignore the needs of the child — social, emotional, and physical." Though Spence recognizes that the challenge is beyond the resources of most schools, he writes that with "strategic linkages and partnerships, schools can reach beyond their walls to obtain additional services, staff, and programs to meet the essential needs of students. . . ."

Spence submits that the benefits to our society in developing schools that care are far-reaching. Such schools can counteract violence, develop social-networking skills, and support the formation of positive school communities. To do this, Spence argues, real-life problems must not be hidden, but consciously confronted.

In our view, Spence's analysis is accurate and timely. We feel that he has "hit the nail on the head," providing a sound and reasoned approach to education which we as a society can use to cultivate and shape the next generation. That approach — innovative and integrative — offers a vision for the future. We expect that it will have an important influence on educational strategies in the years ahead.

The Honourable Justice Roy R. McMurtry
Chief Justice of Ontario (Retired)

The Honourable Justice Michael H. Tulloch
Superior Court of Justice

Introduction: The Promise Offered by Community Schools

Over the course of my career in education — as a teacher, principal, and director of education— I have had the opportunity to see what works in our schools and what does not. This book is the distillation of my thoughts on the subject. It does not pretend to be comprehensive, or to offer the last word on what is admittedly a complex subject. What it does offer is a primer on why our schools need to show CARE — to embrace the principles of Caring, Accepting, Respecting, and Engaging — and how that transformation can be achieved.

I believe deeply in the potential of every child so am saddened to hear of students I taught committing crimes and demonstrating little regard for themselves, their peers, and their community. It was troubling and demoralizing to walk through a detention centre and see too many kids that I taught and too many that looked like me. It was confusing to see them wear their locked-up status as a badge of honour. For many, their introduction to the criminal justice system has become a rite of passage to their manhood. How twisted is that? Their poor choices are life altering and have severe consequences. Because of improper guidance, these youth are wreaking havoc on others, with little thought to where their actions will lead.

At-risk behavior originates in early childhood and elementary school, and in the school setting, it is manifested in low achievement patterns, high absenteeism, low self-esteem, and a variety of other problems. Unchecked, the destructive cycle accelerates; low achievement leads to lower self-esteem and educational disengagement, and significantly increases the likelihood that students will not complete their high school education. Despite the significant resources now directed at these problems, clearly more needs to be done.

The reality is that, despite our best efforts, children face many challenges. Poverty remains high. Many children are likely to be raised in single-parent households. Many young people engage in risky sexual behavior and become pregnant. Some participate in delinquent activities and violence; some use tobacco, alcohol, and drugs. And some suffer from educational problems and fail to meet academic standards (Dryfoos 1997). In the face of these challenges, working together is critical.

Improving student outcomes requires a change in thinking, one that goes beyond the conventional goal of "school improvement." This change in thinking must recognize the reality that more and more families cannot fully meet the multiple needs that must be met if their children are to enjoy academic success.

Schools on their own cannot — and should not — be expected to enable families to meet these needs. Many of these challenges can be better addressed by a *community schools* approach. As the U.S.-based Coalition for Community Schools puts it:

> No matter how great the challenges, schools & communities can pool their resources to help children achieve. [Community schools] — with a focus on academics, health, and social services — offer the most promise for ensuring that every child can succeed, and that we spend precious public dollars as efficiently & effectively as possible. Schools can and should be the centers of every community.

A school that CAREs — as in Caring, Accepting, Respecting, and Engaging — represents both a place and a partnership approach that mobilizes resources, services, supports, and opportunities leading to improved student learning, stronger families, and healthier communities.

Leadership Focused on Relationships

Leadership in the future will be about the creation and maintenance of relationships: the relationships of children to learning, children to children, children to adults, adults to adults, and school to community. It will have to address the increasing complexity of our society, the deterioration of families, and the loss of social capital available to support children and families. It will involve adeptly creating a web of support around children and their families.

School leaders can no longer wait until children are five years old to become involved with their learning. Much research has demonstrated that the early years of a child's life are crucial. If schools wait to address a child's needs past those formative years, the subsequent work becomes much more difficult.

Schools cannot forget about children after 3 p.m. or their work will be diluted. Children spend the bulk of their time some place other than school. Schools can help shape that time through parent education and after-school and summer-learning opportunities. Schools must become part of the broader social context that creates a true system of lifelong learning in the community. Although they need not become all things to all people, they can team up with other care-giving agencies, such as the health department, the parks and recreation officials, or perhaps the church down the street. Together, they can see to it that children and their families are within a network of mutual care.

The key point is that we can no longer pretend that learning stops and starts at the schoolhouse door. Learning has always been affected by the contextual issues that plague many children and families, but we have not always recognized this. We must become courageous champions for children, using our skills to muster the broad support that will enable children to learn successfully. We will also have to make sure that the content of learning changes dramatically. Yes, we will have to create conditions that prepare children for school — but we will also have to create conditions that prepare schools for children.

Schools That Children Want to Attend

Effective school reform focuses on creating schools that students want to go to. These schools have to be places that show CARE — Caring, Accepting, Respecting, and Engaging their students — and that allow learners to undertake activities they find meaningful. Creating such schools requires a total revamping of how we approach teaching and learning. It also requires leaders who are focused on the process. We have to structure learning that speaks to the hearts and minds of learners.

Creating these schools requires us to open them to the broader world. Meaningful learning can happen only in the broadest possible context. Once again, the future will demand that we turn the current process inside out and structure learning so that students can use complex skills in situations that challenge their thinking while connecting them to reality.

We have the chance to reshape the lives of children in profound ways.

We can create a sense of community. That is, we can develop a set of interactions, of human behaviors that have meaning and raise expectations between members. There is not just action, but actions based on shared expectations, values, beliefs, and meanings between individuals where none existed before.

We can transform institutions of learning through our leadership and courage.

A Broader Definition of Student Success

As educators, we recognize that investing in quality education is essential if we are to prepare our children for employment, healthy lifestyles, and responsible citizenship. If young people are to develop the skills needed to live as responsible adults, however, our investment in them must transcend the traditional focus on cognitive development. We must broaden our understanding of education to encompass their continuing intellectual, physical, emotional, and social development and well-being. We cannot ignore the full range of learning needs — social, emotional, and physical. We must redefine what we mean by "student success."

Schools that show CARE build on the idea that both academic and non-academic competencies are important and related to long-range learning outcomes (Pittman and Cahill 1992). What young people know and can do, how they think of themselves, and how they approach the world are intimately connected to their ability to succeed — not just in school, but later in life as citizens, as workers, and as family members. These schools may see the challenge as beyond their existing resources, but they do not see it as outside their core mission.

Options and support for students have already increased through our evolving education system; however, the external factors that also affect a young person's chances need to be addressed. Poor health, inadequate housing, family disorganization, inadequate nutrition, poverty, substance abuse, insufficient childcare, and unsafe streets all hinder our children's development. With their strategic use of linkages and partnerships, schools that CARE can reach beyond their walls to obtain additional services, staff, and programs to meet the essential needs of students and their families, and enhance the range and quality of their learning.

Access to more resources and the active involvement of community partners will support and enhance efforts to address the facts of life that affect both teaching and learning. These include changing demographics, too much unstructured time for some children who lack access to after-school activities and out-of-school opportunities, transience, violence, and unaddressed basic needs. If every school community collaborated with agencies, institutions, and individuals who influence the lives of children and their families, and if the community responded readily to its cultural, ethnic, and economic diversity, then it could streamline efforts to meet the needs of children and their families while involving them in planning what services will be offered and how they will be delivered.

This kind of approach means providing services at places and times that are convenient to families. We must strive to respond to families in crisis, but we must also focus on preventing serious problems by providing positive development opportunities for all children. Support systems must be built or restructured to meet young people's basic developmental needs and to respond to specific problems of children and families in trouble. Problems that confront parents often affect their children — and the converse can be true, as well. Even if multiple services are available to a particular family member, these services may not help if the needs of other family members go unmet.

The principle of equity is fundamental to the concept of public education. *Equity* means ensuring equal access to the benefits that the system has to offer, possibly through differentiated treatment of students. The five goals of educational equity are (1) high academic achievement; (2) equitable access and inclusion; (3) equitable treatment; (4) equitable opportunity to learn; and (5) equitable resources. Equity in education seeks to eliminate systemic barriers to learning — especially social or cultural factors such as race, class, and primary language — and to discover and cultivate the unique gifts, talents, and interests that every human being possesses.

Inner-city schools deal with systemic barriers, especially poverty, daily. As defined by the Toronto District School Board, inner-city schools are schools with a large concentration of students living in poverty. Student learning is affected not only by poverty but by such disparate social factors as culture shock, family status, and youth violence. The problems confronting inner-city schools may include crime, hunger, transience, prostitution, homelessness, emotional neglect, single-parent families, physical and sexual abuse, English as a second language, delayed language development, social and cultural barriers, violence in the home and community, refugee/immigrant status, drug and/or alcohol dependency, fetal alcohol or drug syndrome, and other special needs. Inner-city schools are the places where the most vulnerable children in our society go to learn.

In an effort to promote equity, some school boards, such as the Toronto District, have responded to inner-city schools with innovative approaches and resources. Focused on selected schools, Toronto's Model Schools for Inner Cities initiative emphasizes implementing innovative teaching and learning practices; providing support services to meet students' social, emotional, and physical needs; establishing the schools as the hearts of their communities, researching and evaluating how the students and programs are doing; and sharing successful practices with other schools. The goal is to level the playing field.

Children do not choose poverty. Many of the children in inner-city schools come to class hungry. Health care, proper diet, and physical fitness are often at minimal levels. For many children, the results are poor health and lack of sustainable energy. However, many of them carry their burdens with resilience and grim determination. There is much to admire in their courage and endurance. These students generally enjoy coming to school, which provides a safe, caring, and respectful environment, and can enable them to construct hopeful futures.

Community Support and Partnerships

Educators and community leaders have operated in silos both institutionally and professionally, even though communities everywhere are looking for ways to create excellence, not just to improve schools. Given that the fates of schools and communities are linked, this divide is curious. Many under-performing schools require more than greater financial resources — they require *community support*. To this end, community partnerships can make critical contributions to school improvement. In schools that show CARE, services, supports, and opportunities lead to improved student learning and to a more deeply engaged community. Students come early and stay late because they want to.

In the pages that follow, I set out my view of the direction in which the educational system must move if it is to meet the needs of our young people and society at large. In the first part, chapters 1 to 3, I discuss the defining characteristics of schools that show CARE; in the second part, chapters 4 to 6, I offer examples of schools, programs, and teachers that exemplify these characteristics. Throughout this book, we will explore how collaborative community partnerships can have an impact on schools.

I hope that *Achieving, Believing, and Caring* will encourage you to work towards transforming your own school into one that shows CARE. Doing so just makes sense.

CHAPTER 1

Students at the Centre

O ur most precious resource is people and their potential to work for the collective betterment of society; however, poverty in its numerous manifestations, most obviously low and unreliable income, wastes this resource and its potential.

The Context: Poverty and Families under Stress

The effects of growing up in poverty, particularly for children raised in socially isolated, economically depressed areas, warrant great concern for us as educators. Typically, these children are raised by a single parent. Too often from the start they are starved of adequate nutrition, adequate health care, and the adequate learning stimulants vital for young minds. Here the evidence is clear that the risks faced by these children are substantial.

My own sense is that we cannot simply load the responsibility on our schools. These children face long odds from day one. In the crucial early years, from conception to age three when the mind is largely forged, these children are shackled.

Let's not kid ourselves: poverty is expensive. Just as it is more costly to treat a disease than to prevent one, it costs more to provide emergency hostels than affordable housing, more to take a child into the care of child welfare agencies than to make sure that families have adequate incomes, and more to cope with school dropouts than to train youth for jobs that the nation needs to fill in the coming years.

We've got too many babies raising babies who don't have the resources or the knowledge of how to take care of their children. We should be mobilizing interventions on the front side of these lives; instead, we spend more on police and prisons on the back end.

This is a tragedy of terrible and costly consequences, in lost hope and lost lives.

A vast body of research on children in poverty shows that impoverished conditions greatly increase the multiplier effect on risk variables — single-parent households, low birth weight, low educational attainment of parents, and so on. Poor children generally receive inferior services that are located in the inner-city, and poor children often have many unmet basic needs. This combination of risk factors makes it nearly impossible to establish cause-and-effect relationships among them. For example, because poor children often lack access to preventive health care, their untreated vision problems are inaccurately diagnosed as reading problems and as a consequence, many are placed in remedial and special education programs.

We recognize that there needs to be political will at all levels of government to address issues of poverty and that there has been some progress.

In Ontario, for example, the provincial government has made several important commitments: it has introduced a new Child Benefit aimed at low-income families, an investment of $2 billion; pledged $45 million to provide basic dental care for about 500 000 low-income workers who cannot afford private insurance; decided to reduce the claw back of the National Child Benefit by $50 a month (as of 2011); and vowed to bring in full-day Junior and Senior Kindergarten, which will eventually free up 42 000 full-time daycare spaces that will help many parents return to work. The idea of full-day Kindergarten is terrific when you consider that every dollar invested in high-quality early care and education saves $7.16 in welfare, special education, and criminal justice costs. Perhaps the most important 2009 move is to appoint a cabinet committee on poverty headed by Children and Youth Services Minister Deb Mathews to develop targets and timetables.

On the federal front, the government has introduced a working income supplement that pays at most $500 annually to singles and $1000 to parents. The strategy should include increases to the Canada Child Tax Benefit and major federal investments in early learning, child care, social housing, and employment insurance.

I am, however, constantly reminded that as stewards of public education, we have a tremendous opportunity as well to make a difference by embracing our moral purpose and ensuring that every student in our system is exposed to a climate of high expectations, caring adults, and an engaging curriculum appropriate to instructional level.

We are uniquely positioned to influence some of the non-financial resources that make such a difference in students' lives.

For example, it costs nothing for us to be appropriate role models. Children who are emotionally impoverished are often forced to assume an adult role early in the absence of positive adult role models in their lives. In those cases, role models outside the family are critical for a child's emotional growth and development. As educators we have a greater influence on students than we can ever imagine. Think about a special teacher who made a great impact on your life and your goals . . .

We have these students in our care for 10 months of the year and six hours a day. We have to believe that we can make a difference. Drawing on Stephen Covey's work, we can say that relationships are successful when emotional deposits are made to the student, emotional withdrawals are avoided, and the students are respected.

Poverty does not mean failure, and education is a way out of poverty, but as educators, we must be relentless in our shift from a pedagogy of poverty — a system that sorts and labels with a subtle persistence of low expectations and boring tasks and that escapes responsibility for learning by blaming others — to a pedagogy of plenty that embraces learning for all.

So, if we are sincere about helping our students, we must also help their *parents* and invest in family literacy. As shown in Statistics

Canada's "Adult Literacy and Life Skills Survey — 2003," published in 2005, 4 out of 10 adult Canadians, ages 16 to 65, struggle with low literacy. Of those nine million Canadians, 15 percent have serious problems dealing with any printed materials. The children of functionally illiterate parents are twice as likely to be illiterate, too. An additional 27 percent of those adults can deal only with simple reading tasks (Statistics Canada, 2005). We must view education as a round-the-clock endeavor that can succeed only when children's home lives are improved.

We are fortunate to live in a great nation, one that is founded upon the principles of justice and equality, of liberty and freedom. But our nation is also imperfect. Inequity and injustice are still firmly entrenched.

We must be honest about the fact that, while our educational system is extraordinary in so many respects, it is riddled with outrageous disparities. Children from low-income and minority communities face unconscionable educational inequities. And what does the future hold for individuals who are constrained by an inadequate education? The research is clear: They are more likely to live their entire lives in poverty, more likely to lack adequate health care, and more likely to be incarcerated.

Do these harsh statistical realities arise because children who happen to be born into low-income communities are inherently less capable than their more affluent peers? Those of us who have worked in the classrooms on the front lines of the achievement gap know that nothing could be more false. The truth is that our students' potential to succeed is nothing less than extraordinary. The critical question of our time, then, is how do we tap that potential and ensure high levels of achievement for all children?

What I believe is that strong teaching and effective school leadership are key and that high expectations, like low expectations, are a self-fulfilling prophecy. I believe that we can eliminate the inequities that still plague our education system. Every day that we allow these inequities to continue, we turn our backs on those who deserve our attention the most.

We have an obligation to make a simple, but powerful commitment to our children. We must promise them that the opportunity to pursue their dreams will be constrained only by the limits of their imaginations, and never by their postal codes. And I believe deeply, with every fibre of my being that we can fulfill this obligation. I believe this because I have found that the achievement gap is ultimately vulnerable to the greatness inherent in all children and to the power of talented, hard-working adults of vision.

The heightened level of accountability, now part of our school-system culture, will not disappear. Nor should the disaggregation of data that allows the monitoring of the performance of student subgroups. Undoubtedly, the most prevalent and persistent gaps exist as a result of poverty. Along the lines of the self-fulfilling prophecy, children of poverty tend to live in low-income neighbourhoods and attend low-income schools where student achievement generally lags behind the performance of students from middle-income and higher income homes. By focusing resources where they are needed most — on schools serving children of poverty — we significantly increase the chances that those resources will help close the achievement gap.

Educators also know that the effects of poverty cannot be totally erased by what we do in school. Teachers can affect the mind and body, but what happens outside of school is also an important part of the equation. Factors such as prenatal care, the health services available to a child after birth, the quality of child care, the availability of preschool programs, and full-day Kindergarten all play a role in affecting a child's ability to learn. These are critical components in the elimination of an achievement gap that exists long before a child ever sets foot in the classroom.

The needs of today's students are many and complex, but institutional response has been uneven.

In general, systems do not respond to early warning signs, but rather react to failure or crisis, when it is much more difficult and expensive to make a change. There is little investment in preventive or developmental services that strengthen the capacities of children and families to help themselves. To make matters worse, most of these systems function in isolation, apart from the education system and each other. Interventions tend to deal with parts of problems, rather than children and families specifically. Schools alone cannot meet the myriad service needs of young people and their families; welfare and social services may momentarily mitigate a crisis, but cannot promise a hopeful future to those who lack the abilities demanded by the job market. Few mechanisms exist to identify those in need and ensure that they are aware of, have access to, and benefit from resources available to help them.

If young people are to flourish, as a society we must do a better job of publicly supporting families and communities as well as institutions such as schools. Our families, communities, and institutions have a combined responsibility not only to meet children's basic needs, such as food, shelter, and access to medical care, and abstract needs like a sense of safety, belonging, and participation in caring relationships, but also to prepare them for a productive and rewarding future.

A **system of learning supports** is a set of supports, internal and external to the school board, that operate cohesively as a comprehensive continuum of actions, programs, and services to support learning for all students in our schools.

It is not the school's responsibility alone to provide rich and varied opportunities for children to develop essential skills and competencies. Learning and development take place and are affected as much by what happens outside school as what occurs inside. All young people need access to developmental opportunities in their homes, neighborhoods, and schools. These opportunities can be provided through organized sports and recreational activities, art, music and cultural enrichment programs, hobbies, volunteer service, and summer jobs.

Some children and families have exceptional needs that may require more intensive responses to ensure ongoing healthy development and success. Young people who are ill or who have physical or mental disabilities, learning disorders, or behavioral problems often need individualized interventions. Families in distress may need financial help as well as assistance in providing shelter, medical care, and comfort and nurturing for their children.

The Goals of a Student-Centred Culture

In schools that show CARE — Caring, Accepting, Respecting, and Engaging — the student is the centre around which all else revolves. A student-centred culture focuses on creating the kinds of learners who have these characteristics: they have clear learning goals; they have a wide repertoire of learning strategies and know when to use them; they use available resources effectively; they know their strengths and weaknesses, understand the learning process, deal appropriately with their feelings, and take responsibility for their own learning; and they plan, monitor, evaluate, and adapt their learning processes.

Harden and Crosby (2000, 335) describe student-centred learning as focusing on the students' learning and "what students do to achieve this, rather than what the teacher does." Their definition emphasizes the concept of the student doing. In contrast, they say that teacher-centred learning strategies focus on the teacher transmitting knowledge from the expert to the novice.

Other authors articulate broader, more comprehensive definitions of student-centred learning. Lea and colleagues (2003, 322) summarize some of the literature, identifying the following tenets:

the reliance on active rather than passive learning,
an emphasis on deep learning and understanding,
increased responsibility and accountability on the part of the student,
an increased sense of autonomy in the learner,
an interdependence between teacher and learner,
mutual respect within the learner–teacher relationship, and
a reflexive approach to the teaching and learning process on the part of both teacher and learner.

Simply put, a student-centred culture tailors all aspects of service delivery and support to the needs of students. It is guided by what is best for the students when helping them or making decisions about their education. While many of us are personally committed to serving students' needs, the structure of our organization and policies may hinder our desire to be more student centred. Creating such a culture means removing administrative barriers and deconstructing the current bureaucracy in order to provide convenient, seamless, high-quality service whenever possible.

Another key goal in a student-centred culture is the development of leadership skills, something that involves students both in and beyond the classroom. This development means providing opportunities for students to demonstrate their talents, skills, and interests while continuing to develop new ones. It is also about giving students more ownership of the programs they attend. One example is the STARS program run by the Hamilton-Wentworth District School Board. STARS stands for Students Taking Action, Reaching Success. The program provides numerous opportunities for students to get involved with leadership and fosters an excellent environment for developing leadership skills.

We need to make a conscious decision to include students in meaningful ways; however, this goal is more easily expressed in words than achieved. It takes time and energy to find ways to include students. It can mean letting go of controlling how and what happens, and being open to new ways of doing things. We can encourage student involvement by supporting and cultivating student councils, which can organize activities, plan student events, conduct student orientations, help solve problems in programs, and much else.

The gains from promoting student involvement can be significant. First and foremost, students can improve and strengthen programs as they bring new energy and ideas to them. Student input also provides opportunities for them to learn skills transferable to the workplace or community. Finally, student input deepens each student's commitment to lifelong learning

An Ethic of Caring

With recent significant social changes, such as the increase in single-parent households, our schools need to become places where an ethic of caring forms the centrepiece of the educational program. Achieving this will not be an easy task, but it is necessary. Next to the home, the majority of students spend most of their time in school. No institution is in a better position to help students become responsible, caring citizens.

Research indicates that one of the most potent factors in deterring violence among our young people is a stable, loving relationship with an adult. Wallach (1993), accordingly, suggests that building such relationships ought to be the top priority in helping children at-risk. Similarly, a study of high-risk children, in which researchers followed the same group for 32 years from birth to adulthood, found one major factor separating those who overcame their pasts from those who did not: supportive relationships with significant adults who "encouraged trust, autonomy and initiative" (Jeary 2001).

Citing earlier studies on love deprivation in infants, Montagu (1970, 466) argued that when a child is not loved, it responds in aggressive ways. "The child learns to love by being loved. When it is not loved it fails to learn to love and responds with protesting behaviour, with rage and aggression."

A Fatherless World

One of the most reliable predictors of whether a boy will succeed or fail in high school rests on a single question: does he have a man in his life to look up to?

Michael Gurian writes, "A boy without a father figure is like an explorer without a map."

Many schools are witnessing a sharp increase in the number of children exhibiting anti-social behavior (see R.D. Stephens in *Helping Students Graduate*). This rise is particularly evident in urban environments where poverty exercises an exacerbating influence (see, for example, Dishion et al. 1995). There students, particularly those living in impoverished conditions, may be exposed to significant within-family and community-based risk factors. Many children in these circumstances hail from large families headed by single parents (most often mothers). One or more of the older siblings may already have had encounters with law enforcement. Making matters worse, these children experience daily decaying neighborhoods and poorly maintained public buildings and family dwellings. For many such children, these conditions exist prior to their entering school and persist throughout their education. As a result, they come to school unskilled and ill prepared to take advantage of learning opportunities offered within a system that has changed little over time to accommodate their needs.

Relationships

Relationships are the foundation upon which all other attributes of a safe and caring school are built. Without a strong foundation of open, caring, and trusting relationships, it will be difficult to promote and strengthen the other dimensions of safe and caring schools. Strong relationships between student and student, between student and teacher, and between teacher and teacher ensure effective communication and support. Relationships help students and staff members learn how to interact with one another and how to create and maintain a peaceful environment. They also help individuals to feel more comfortable when moving from class to class.

Many different strategies can be used to build and achieve strong relationships. Here are several examples:

spirit week	theme days
pep rallies	parent volunteers
student announcements	school sweaters
buddy system between different grade-level students	awards and recognition of student achievement
stress-buster week	involvement of community
peer support program	agencies (e.g., law enforce-
interschool track meet	ment and social work) in the
dances organized by students	school
mixed-grade homerooms	provision of a variety of
house leagues	programs that appeal to
mixed sports teams	diverse student populations

A caring, supportive relationship is one of the most powerful factors available to protect young people from negative influences. Meaningful interaction between adults and youth builds mutual respect and provides young people with mentors and positive role models (Benard 1996). The disciplining of our children is inextricably linked to the basic values we hold as human beings. Those values will guide us in the writing of our laws and in the codes of conduct that we establish in our schools.

The Canadian National Crime Prevention Council (1995) embraced this positive philosophy in its paper "Clear Limits and Real Opportunities: The Keys to Preventing Youth Crime." In the same vein, MacDonald (e.g., 1999), in her study of Junior High schools in Alberta, argues against "chasing the storm clouds: and, instead, seeing discipline as an opportunity to teach social skills rather than punish wrongdoers." She shows, in a practical way, how the conceptualization of discipline and violence influences the behavior of school principals, one of the key players in the school process.

Other studies report that there are significant differences in the perceptions held by students, teachers, and administrators about school violence (see MacDonald and Da Costas 1996). While educators, parents, and others may see the levels of violence in school as disturbing, students may have come to see such behavior as "normal." Consequently, they may be unwilling to report the majority of incidents for fear of reprisals or being outside the prevailing norms (MacDonald 1997a).

Understanding Boys At-Risk

A growing problem in our society is with our boys. All around us we can see evidence of increasing alienation, anger, violence, and under-achievement among boys. Sometimes, parents may wonder if it is possible to raise their sons to become strong, sensitive, and successful. The transition from boyhood to manhood can be complicated.

The academic and social challenges that confront our boys in school settings suggest an urgent need for programmed intervention on the part of educators. Such initiatives should focus on helping our boys develop the attitudes, skills, behaviors, and values necessary to perform at optimal levels at school and in society. We must also recognize that the variation between boys can be large. Too often, we deal with generalities without recognizing the diversity in our students; therefore, the question "Which boys?" is valid. Failure by concerned educators to ask the question will lead to a blanket one-size-fits-all approach to reform, effectively silencing the experiences and needs of many students. Because of past experience, boys from minority populations may have less faith in the education system than do students from more enfranchised groups.

Males of Color At-Risk

Black males are more likely

- to be suspended or expelled
- to drop out
- to be placed in special education
- to be missing from honors, gifted, and advanced placement
- to be under-represented among school staff

The decline of fatherhood is one of the most basic and extraordinary social trends of our time. No one predicted this trend. Few researchers or government agencies have monitored it and it is not widely discussed. But the decline of fatherhood is a major force behind many of the most disturbing problems that plague society: crime and delinquency, deteriorating educational achievement, depression, substance abuse and alienation among adolescents, and the growing number of women and children in poverty.

The most tangible and immediate consequence of fatherlessness for children is the loss of economic resources. The income of the household in which a child remains after a divorce instantly declines, while expenses tend to go up. Over time, the economic situation for the child often worsens. The mother usually earns considerably less than the father, and children cannot rely on their fathers to pay much in the way of child support.

I do know this: boys are more likely to achieve and have a positive outlook on life if they have men to look up to. Dads are the best possible role models as long as they give their sons appropriate messages and take the time to be with them. When good dads are *not* around, moms and teachers need to search elsewhere. Male teachers, mentors, and coaches can make a difference.

Our society dictates that men spend long hours away from home working. On average, fathers spend about 10 minutes a day with their children (less than a minute with infants and one hour with adolescents). Of course, mothers can also be effective role models and mentors to boys, but boys seem to need to reassure themselves of their own masculinity. While growing up, they feel a certain pressure not only to appear masculine but also not to appear feminine. Boys with such perceived feminine characteristics as tenderness, compassion, and empathy are often considered soft or emotionally vulnerable. They may be targeted for ridicule.

Economic difficulties, which translate into poorer schooling and other setbacks, ultimately account for a large share of the disadvantages found among fatherless children. One authoritative study of this problem is *Growing Up with a Single Parent* (1994), by sociologists Sara McLanahan of Princeton University and Gary Sandefur of the University of Wisconsin. Reviewing five large-scale social surveys and other evidence (and after adjusting for many income-related factors), they conclude: "Children who grow up with only one of their biological parents (nearly always the mother) . . . are twice as likely to drop out of high school, 2.5 times as likely to become teen mothers and 1.4 times as likely to be idle — out of school and out of work — as children who grow up with both parents."

Fathers — and fatherlessness — have surprising impacts on children. Fathers' involvement seems to be linked to improved quantitative and verbal skills, improved problem-solving ability, and higher academic achievement. Several studies have found that the presence of the father is one determinant of girls' proficiency in mathematics, and one study discovered that the amount of time fathers spent reading was a strong predictor of their daughters' verbal ability. For sons, who can more directly follow their fathers' example, the results have been even more striking.

Studies have uncovered a strong relationship between father involvement and the quantitative and mathematical abilities of their sons. Other studies have found a relationship between paternal nurturing and boys' verbal intelligence. Fathers who spent time alone with their children more than twice a week, giving meals, baths, and other basic care, reared the most compassionate adults.

Again, it is not yet clear why fathers are so important in instilling this quality. Perhaps merely by being with their children, they provide a model of compassion. Perhaps it has to do with their style of play or mode of reasoning. Perhaps it somehow relates to the fact that fathers typically are the family's main arbiters with the outside world. Whatever the reason, it is hard to think of a more important contribution that fathers can make to their children.

As for mothers, they must reclaim their right to shape their sons — without worrying about turning them into that worst-of-all-possible male: the "mama's boy." Many mothers accept the idea that they need to cut the cord with their sons to turn them into men ready to take on masculine roles in the world, from achieving material success to making war. The deep emotional connection between a mother and her son has been demonized for generations.

Some contend that parents treat their male and female children differently and that this inconsistency causes differences in the behavior of boys and girls. It is true that, when adults do not know a particular infant or child, they tend to respond to the youngster on the basis of sex. This makes good sense. Adults are relying on their knowledge about what boys and girls are typically like in the absence of information about the particular child they encounter.

Boys who seriously misbehave in school frequently commit crimes out of school. Aggressive behavior is a precursor and predictor of school dropout rates, anti-social behavior, delinquency and criminality, and suicides. It is clearly in the interest of boys — and of the rest of us who must raise, support, and develop them — to address destructive aggression early.

No one disputes that there is a male–female disparity in levels of aggression. This difference remains constant across time, cultures, and species. Evolutionary psychologists trace the difference to the male role of hunter and protector. We see this difference acted out in the universal fondness that boys, but not girls, have for rough-and-tumble play. Adults often try to discourage this kind of play, but boys nevertheless persist in it when not being monitored.

While substantial male–female differences exist in levels of activity and aggression, it is also true that certain kinds of family environments can exaggerate aggressive behavior in boys. Families of aggressive boys employ confrontation instead of negotiation to resolve conflicts. As a result of this disciplinary approach, aggressive boys tend to interpret the intentions of others as malicious, when they are not.

Once a pattern of aggression is established, it often leads to other problems. Parenting practices per se are not the best predictor of adolescent and adult problems, such as delinquency, criminality, and dropout rates. Rather, the level of childhood aggression predicts these outcomes. Early styles of parenting can reinforce a pattern of aggression in childhood, which, in turn, encourages later forms of destructive behavior.

Over the last decade, for every Black male enrolled in college, six Black males join the prison and jail population. One in three African American males are involved in the penal system. It is estimated that by 2020, over 65 percent of African American males, ages 20 to 29, will be involved in some form of the penal system.

No boys are at greater risk than those in the Black community. "One out of twenty-one Black American males will be murdered in their lifetime. Most will die at the hands of another Black man." These two quoted statements, the second following the first on a black background, introduce *Boyz N the Hood*, a 1991 Columbia Pictures film about three young Blacks growing up in south-central Los Angeles, written and directed by John Singleton. Singleton's film does not offer an explanation for its opening statements, but it does elaborate on the brutal conditions this crisis entails. More significantly, *Boyz* offers an alternative vision, not so much about how to address violence in the community as how to get out of it. More than merely strategic or pragmatic, this vision is also a principled guide to living one's life.

Another film, *Baby Boy* (Columbia Pictures 1991), depicts Black men trapped in a state of perpetual emotional infancy. They call their women "mama," their friends "my boys," and their place "the crib." Jody is a classic example of this. Despite being 20 years old and having fathered two children by different women, Jody has been unable to cut the strings to his childhood and become a mature adult. His story is that of many young Black men trapped by limited economic potential and uncertain family ties.

These films are just a couple of examples of our society's concern about the declining social, economic, and educational status of young Black males. The host of problems besetting this group — high unemployment, extensive violence, and criminal activity (including homicide), disproportionate representation in the criminal justice system, and last-place ranking on many measures of educational performance and attainment — have led many to conclude that the future of young Black males is dismal.

Still, measures are being taken to address these concerns. For example, in Canada, the 9 Heavens Healing Academy, led by Curtis Bell, mandates the eradication of gang/gun violence by assisting participants through the healing process, so that they can become healthy parents and productive law-abiding members of their communities. The academy is committed to reclaiming, restoring, and healing youth in the Jane and Finch corridor in Toronto. By building young people's confidence and positive self-image, staff provide them with hope for their future. 9 Heavens is confident that given the opportunity at the academy, youth will flourish and expand their abilities beyond that which they previously believed.

9 Heavens elicits similarities between inner-city life and life on Native Canadian reserves. It expands participants' frame of reference beyond city streets. Tangible approaches to promoting responsibility and life skills development include relocation of youth to Grand River County where participants benefit from new experiences that emphasize healing and nature. Participants grow towards wholeness and can even achieve spiritual cleansing by experiencing Aboriginal traditions. By attending the 9 Heavens Healing Academy, young men begin to realize their true potential in life and endeavor to engage in a positive and productive passage into manhood.

One important reason why young Blacks find themselves in this dire situation is the absence of fathers in their lives. The landmark 1965 Moynihan Report found that one key factor that had led to the deterioration of the Black family was the high proportion of Black families headed only by females (see Pinkney 1987 and Staples 1986). The report blames Blacks rather than society and fails to recognize that racism perpetuates unequal opportunities and the overrepresentation of Blacks among the poor. It also masks the relationship between poverty and family stability regardless of race. For both these reasons, the Moynihan Report is problematic; however, it did raise what remains a pressing issue: How *does* a boy come of age in our fast-paced, information-overloaded, materialistic society? Most important, what role do adults play in helping boys assume the mantle of manhood?

Getting past the risk factors

I believe that our generally accepted standard for what it means to be a man is a poor guide. If I were to follow that guide, I would never reveal an emotion other than anger; I would idolize, depend on, then denigrate women; I would get into sports, then booze, then money. I did a lot of that in my younger years and it did not make me a man. When I was a teenager, you achieved no glory unless you could consume and keep down, large quantities of alcohol. Being successful with girls, especially pretty ones, was also an accomplishment. No real prestige was achieved unless you could also hit a fastball over the fence or make a jump shot.

Over time, I came to a better understanding of how a boy becomes a man, but not on my own. My parents showed me how I could take care of myself. They showed me how to think about other people without judging or criticizing them when they did things differently. They showed me how to be responsible and not to take things so personally. They showed me how to love. They showed me how to become a man.

Who Is a Student At-Risk?

Bailey and Stegelin (2003) define a student at risk as "someone who is unlikely to graduate on schedule with both the skills and the self-esteem necessary to exercise meaningful options in the areas of work, leisure, culture, civic affairs, and inter/intrapersonal relationships."

Status variables include age and gender; socioeconomic background; ethnicity; native language; mobility; and family structure.

Alterable variables include grades and retention; disruptive behavior; absenteeism; school policies and climate; sense of belonging; attitude towards school; and support in the home.

Boys at-risk need someone to show them these things, as well.

Maxims on Becoming a Man

Becoming a man means having integrity, of being complete or undivided, especially when it comes to moral and ethical values. It means leading a principle-centred life.

Becoming a man means keeping your word. As Mark Twain put it: "When you tell the truth, you don't have to remember anything."

Becoming a man means doing the right thing. Sometimes, doing the right thing is a hard thing to do. It means doing right when no one is around to make you do right.

Becoming a man means having the courage and the mental or moral strength to venture or persevere and withstand danger, fear, opposition, and hardship. It does not mean that you are never afraid.

Becoming a man means being humble. A truly thankful man is humble — he knows from whom the blessings in life come.

Becoming a man means being motivated intrinsically rather than extrinsically. A man does what he does because of the reward of inward peace.

Becoming a man means helping those who need help, bringing hope to the hopeless.

Becoming a man means trying to get along with your parents and understanding the role they played in raising you.

Becoming a man means finding people whom you can call friends. Support them and help them whenever necessary. Do so selflessly and without desire for any return.

Becoming a man means finding that special someone. Learn from that person and give love in return.

Becoming a man means giving back. Do something, anything, to give back to the community in which you live. Understand that you are blessed with the ability to make a difference.

Being a man is more than turning a certain age, maybe 13, 18, or 21. It involves having the courage to be open to who you are as you continue your life journey.

All of the above maxims are ones that our education system, by following the principles of a student-centred culture in the context of schools that show CARE, should strive to inculcate in our youth. Their future, and ours, depends upon it.

Zero Tolerance versus Caring Alternatives

There has been much talk about the need for "zero tolerance" in our schools when it comes to various forms of anti-social behavior, particularly violence. Increasingly, however, educators are coming to realize that zero tolerance is too inflexible a tool to deal effectively with inappropriate conduct. Not only does it offer school authorities little or no room for discretion in its application, but it assumes a black-and-white, blanket approach to problems that are best addressed on a case-by-case basis, in the interests both of the students involved and of the larger community.

Effective alternatives to "zero tolerance" should involve students, families, and their communities in efforts to provide a safe learning environment and safety in school. Anti-violence programs, like anti-bullying, anger management, and peer mediation, help to reduce discipline problems in schools. These promising programs have been developed and are being implemented in many schools. They should be copied elsewhere.

One such program is YAAACE, or Youth Association for Academics Athletics and Character Education, an organization founded by Devon Thompson and Devon Jones. YAAACE'S mandate is to create a culture of high academic achievement and social and civic responsibility among its members and establish an infrastructure that will bridge the gap between young people north and south of Finch (polarized due to gang involvement). In recent years, the United Way of Greater Toronto listed Jane and Finch as one of nine neighborhoods that are severely impoverished, have limited access to services, and face significant challenges. Jane-Finch is one of 13 at-risk Toronto communities targeted by the mayor of Toronto's community safety plan which aims to provide solutions to gun-related violence.

Relationships Matter

You can't motivate a student you don't know. There is no learning without trust and respect, and today's students do not grant either automatically — they must be earned.

YAAACE strives to forge meaningful partnerships with parents, mentors, and organizations with whom youth interact. It has partnered with institutions such as the Toronto District and Catholic District school boards, York University, Seneca College, Ryerson University, Department of Justice, and many other agencies and community organizations. It applies proactive strategies to facilitate social and academic engagement, thereby combating gang subculture and low academic achievement in the neighborhood.

Three reports — Roots of Youth Violence, the Colour of Poverty Campaign, and the joint Toronto District School Board and Ministry of Education Staff Report (January 2008) — collectively document the systemic underachievement of certain vulnerable demographic groups of students and speak to concerns and alternatives to engage them socially and academically. Their findings reinforce the value of YAAACE'S mandate. YAAACE addresses academic involvement, in part through tutoring; elite athletic involvement, including the development of teamwork; character education, such as promotion of core ethical values; and the Youth March Break and Summer institutes, or camps.

At the same time, the best ways to respond to problems of discipline in school are building student–teacher relationships, offering a challenging curriculum, and providing teacher training in classroom management. Such efforts make schools safer and more equitable while also promoting learning. So do programs for at-risk youth that adhere to a set of basic principles:

- high expectations for all;
- clear, achievable goals;
- clear rules for behavior, fairly enforced;
- effective instruction and classroom management;
- careful monitoring of student progress; and
- emphasis on the school's role as a place for learning.

Research done on the hallmarks of effective schools strongly demonstrates that such schools establish and maintain high expectations and standards for all students and focus on helping them meet those expectations. At-risk youth are often channelled into programs with special, reduced expectations for performance, especially academic performance. This practice is misguided.

At-risk youth exhibit both a lack of and a strong need for success. With clear goals and objectives, they can move towards and achieve measurable success in school. At the same time, lack of consistency in discipline often contributes to their problems. The research supports the establishment and maintenance of clear rules for behavior of all students, with behavior measured against those rules — *not* against previous behavior or the behavior of other students — and with rules enforced fairly and equitably for all.

A problem in schools with high at-risk populations is the decline of student engagement and the performance of these students. Effective classroom instruction and management techniques, with emphasis on teacher responsibility and the expectation that all students can and will learn, may counteract this trend. Attention must also be paid to the needs of individual at-risk students, who typically lack engagement in learning. In this regard, the research supports the careful monitoring of all students' progress, with teacher interventions whenever necessary to improve student learning. It also emphasizes the value of involving students in their own learning and instilling understanding of and respect for the fact that school is a place dedicated to learning.

The accumulated knowledge of alternative programs for at-risk young people — see Chapter 5 — seems to support substantially the findings and recommendations of the research into effective schools. The differences between the two seem principally to concern curriculum goals or purposes of education. Nonetheless, given the set of goals professed by each "side," the means of attaining them show great congruence. The conclusion to which this analysis points can be summed up in the words of Ronald Edmonds (1979, 23): "We can, whenever and wherever we choose, successfully teach all children whose schooling is of interest to us; we already know more than we need to do that; and whether or not we do it must finally depend on how we feel about the fact that we haven't so far."

Practices That Serve Students' Best Interests

In schools that show CARE, there is a close correlation between school and teacher practices and student achievement. The practices that such schools observe on their journeys to excellence can be summarized as follows:

- visualizing their learning communities as ones that are compassionate and inclusive, that value, foster, and support learning, that provide relevant resources and opportunities and that have a vision and shared goals;
- visualizing their learners as individuals who assume responsibility for learning, become lifelong learners, have a variety of learning needs and needs different from other learners, need a variety of experiences and opportunities, learn independently and with others, and balance working and playing; and
- supporting their learners by being responsive, adaptable, respectful of diversity, empowering, accessible, and linked to the community.

There are several keys to serving students' best interests: providing support for student learning; knowing the students; knowing the curriculum; knowing the learning environment; treating students and staff with a sense of equity and respect; holding high expectations of students; assessing and evaluating students effectively, making integrated use of technology; showing evidence of planning and preparation; promoting teamwork; fostering ongoing professional development; communicating with parents; promoting extracurricular involvement; managing classrooms effectively; and demonstrating commitment towards the students.

Underlying all of these practices, of course, is the principle of caring. Schools that show CARE keep in mind the fundamental truth that their purpose is to serve the best interests of those under their charge. Sensitivity to their individual needs, awareness of the pressures that bear upon them in the larger community, and, above all, a commitment to fostering a sense of responsibility in students for their own education are what make these schools successful.

We should learn from them.

CHAPTER 2

A Vision for Teaching and Learning

In schools that show CARE, the teaching and learning process is central. Such schools enable all members of the learning community to engage in meaningful and challenging experiences and opportunities, the result of which is the creation of individuals who will be well equipped to master complex problems and address pressing social issues.

Great teachers are prepared and organized. They are in their classrooms early and ready to teach. They present lessons in a clear and structured way. Their classrooms are organized in such a manner as to minimize distractions.

Great teachers also engage students and get them to look at issues in a variety of ways. They use facts as a starting point, not as an end point; they ask "why" questions, look at all sides of issues, and encourage students to predict what will happen next. They try to involve the whole class, rather than allowing a few students to dominate the discussion. They keep students motivated with varied, lively approaches to learning.

Recognition That All Children Are Different

See Chapter 6 for profiles of several outstanding teachers who show CARE.

But teachers who show CARE must do even more than this, crucial though it is. In the first place, they must recognize some basic truths — one of which is that no two children are alike (see Tomlinson and McTighe 2006; Good 2006; and Tomlinson 2005).

- No two children learn in the identical way. In the classroom we should teach children to think for themselves.
- One way is to group children so that they are talking to each other, asking questions of each other, learning to be teachers. One of the most important concepts for a five-year-old to know is that he or she can teach because you have to understand something to teach it.

Differentiated learning: Great minds don't think alike

Hence, learning must be differentiated to be effective. Differentiating instruction means creating multiple paths so that students of different abilities, interests, or learning needs experience equally appropriate ways to absorb, use, develop, and present concepts as a part of daily learning. It allows students to take greater responsibility and ownership for their own learning, and provides opportunities for peer teaching and cooperative learning.

There are generally several students in any classroom who are working below or above grade level, and these levels of readiness will vary between different subjects in school. It is important to offer students tasks that are appropriate to their learning needs rather than just to the grade and subject. Doing this means providing three or four different options — not 35 — for students in any given class. Readiness (ability), learning styles, and interests vary between students and even within an individual over time. In a differentiated classroom, all students have equally engaging learning tasks.

In a school that shows CARE, the teacher prepares for this kind of instruction by diagnosing the differences in readiness, interests, and learning styles of all students in the class, using a variety of performance indicators. Students with specific needs should be presented with learning activities that offer opportunities for developing skills as well as opportunities to display individual strengths. More advanced students may do activities with inherently higher-level thinking requirements and greater complexity.

Instruction Infused with Care

No less important than differentiated instruction is instruction infused with a teacher's care for his or her students. Several longitudinal and ethnographic studies reveal that youth of all ages want a teacher who cares about them (Benard 1995). One observes that "the number of student references to wanting caring teachers is so great that we believe it speaks to the quiet desperation and loneliness of many adolescents in today's society" (Phelan, Davidson, and Cao 1992). Students work harder, achieve more, and attribute more importance to schoolwork in classes in which they feel liked, accepted, and respected by the teacher and fellow students. The caring classroom is not one that avoids criticism, challenges, or mistakes. Rather, it makes every member feel valued and important. This sense of belonging allows for lively, critical discussions and intellectual risk taking. It provides an important source of motivation to do one's best. Research on the development of an individual's self-image suggests that a classroom climate that is warm and accepting of students' feelings enhances pro-social behavior and academic achievement (Rutter 1983).

The vision for teaching and learning at the heart of schools that show CARE, therefore, encompasses

- setting and attaining high standards for teaching and learning;
- providing adequate time for learning, collaboration, and self-reflection;
- offering learning activities that are global, collaborative, integrated, "real world," and hands-on;
- providing opportunities to learn in diverse ways according to individual needs;

"Too often we underestimate the power of a touch, a smile, a kind word, a listening ear, an honest compliment, or the smallest act of caring, all of which we have the potential to turn around."

— Leo Buscaglia in *The Starbucks Experience*

Teachers, coaches, and mentors contribute to the academic awakenings of students by engaging them in regular conversations about their hopes, dreams, and aspirations; recognizing student accomplishments that indicate beyond-the-self concerns; linking school activities with students' life plans; probing for deeper thinking by frequently asking, Why?; connecting school lessons to larger world issues; and providing students with the pedagogical reasons behind an activity or lesson.

From a Student Perspective

Am I being challenged?
Do I feel sense of ownership and
    pride here?
Can I talk to you, the teacher?
Will I feel confident to go to the
    next phase of my life?
Do they care about me?
Do I feel connected and welcome
    here?

- creating a caring and supportive learning environment and a climate that encourages self-expression and risk taking;
- giving attention to the development of such qualities as initiative, persistence, and responsibility;
- developing communication and interaction in the learning community; and
- celebrating student achievement.

A supportive teacher–student relationship is critical to school success (Brophy and Good 1986). School programs with positive teacher–student relationships — particularly ones that help the student feel connected to a learning community — have successfully reduced the dropout rate (M. Fine 1986). Accordingly, schools should hire and retain teachers not only with expertise in their respective roles but also with the following qualities:

- support of and commitment to the school's vision, beliefs, and values;
- high expectations for students and the willingness to work both collaboratively and one on one to create conditions that promote student success;
- ability to operate supportive mentoring programs;
- thorough knowledge of the curriculum and willingness to follow it;
- commitment to collaborative curriculum planning and decision making, focusing on continuity across grade levels and subject areas;
- willingness to utilize a variety of strategies that foster engaged learning to enhance student learning and success;
- understanding of effective assessment tools and skills;
- concern for each student's needs, learning styles, and interests;
- classroom management skills that optimize learning, use time effectively, promote self-worth, and emphasize full participation; and
- instructional techniques that foster thinking skills and creative problem solving.

Teachers Connecting with Students

See "Breakfast and the Walk-in Closet, Hamilton," in Chapter 5 as an example of how schools have implemented programs to help meet students' basic needs.

Teachers — and when I say teachers, I am referring to caring adults who work at the school, be they principals, teachers, or support staff — should be, first and foremost, caring individuals who develop relationships with their students. Through trust and respect, they should convey the message that they are "there for" a youth. To the greatest extent possible, they should help meet the basic survival needs of overwhelmed students and their families. On a more comprehensive level, they may connect students and their families to outside community resources in order to find food, shelter, clothing, counselling, treatment, and mentoring.

Providing connection also translates into meeting emotional safety needs. Resilient survivors talk about teachers' "quiet availability," "fundamental positive regard," and "simple sustained kindness," such as a smile or a greeting (Higgins 1994, 324–25). Being interested in, actively listening to, and validating the feelings of struggling young people, as well as getting to know their strengths and gifts, convey the message, "You matter." According to renowned urban educator Deborah Meier (1995, 120), this kind of respect — having a person "acknowledge us, see us for who we are, as their equal in value and importance" — figures high in caring relationships.

Such teachers connect with their students by showing compassion — non-judgmental support that looks beneath the students' negative behavior and sees their pain and suffering. They do not take students' behavior personally, no matter how negative it may be, but understand instead that students are doing the best possible, given their experiences. As Noddings (1998, 32) points out, "it is obvious that children will work harder and do things — even odd things like adding fractions — for people they love and trust."

At the core of caring relationships are positive and high expectations that not only structure and guide behavior but also challenge students to perform beyond what they believe they can manage. These expectations reflect a deep belief in a student's innate competence. A consistent description of turnaround teachers/mentors is that they see the possibility of each student: "They held visions of us that we could not imagine for ourselves" (Delpit 1996, 199).

Turnaround teachers

"Youth are resources to be developed not problems to be fixed."

— Prof. Robert Blum

Turnaround teachers/mentors, however, not only see the possibilities; they also recognize existing competencies and mirror them back, helping students appreciate where they are already strong. When they use these strengths, interests, goals, and dreams as the beginning point for learning, they tap the students' intrinsic motivation and innate drive to learn. Positive and high expectations then become easier for students to meet.

This identification of strengths can especially assist overwhelmed, labeled, and oppressed youth in reframing their narratives from "damaged victims" to "resilient survivors." Turnaround teachers/mentors help youth to avoid the temptation to take personally the adversity in their lives ("You aren't the cause of — nor can you control — your father's drinking"), to see adversity as permanent ("This too shall pass — your future will be different") and to view setbacks as pervasive ("You can rise above this"). Believing in our students' resilience requires foremost that we believe in our own innate capacity to transform and change.

Teachers who show CARE build their students' sense of competency by teaching metacognition — the understanding of how thoughts influence feelings and behaviors. When students recognize their own conditioned thinking — the environmental messages they have internalized that they are not good enough, smart enough, thin enough, and so on — they can remove blocks to their innate resilience.

Rutter and his colleagues (1984) found a striking similarity between effective urban schools in poor communities — schools in which the rates of delinquency and dropping out declined the longer students were enrolled. All of the schools gave students "a lot of responsibility. Students participated very actively in all sorts of things that went on in the school: they were treated as responsible people and they reacted accordingly" (65). Indeed, providing outlets for student contribution is a natural outgrowth of working from this strengths-based perspective. In a physically and psychologically safe and structured environment, opportunities for participation may include asking questions that encourage self-reflection; encouraging critical thinking and dialogue (especially on salient social and personal issues); making learning more experimental; helping others through community service, peer assistance, and cooperative learning; involving students in curriculum planning and giving them choices in their learning experiences; using participatory evaluation strategies; and involving students in creating the governing rules of the classroom.

Even in classroom discipline issues, student participation can have surprising benefits. "Bring the kids in on it!" Alfie Kohn (1993, 14) urges. "Instead of reaching for coercion, engage children and youth in a conversation about the underlying causes of what is happening and work together to negotiate a solution." When we invite students to help create the classroom rules and school policies, we ensure their "buy in," ownership, and sense of belonging. Perhaps more important, we build their ability to make responsible choices. "It is in the classrooms and families where participation is valued above adult control that students have the chance to learn self-control," writes Kohn (18).

The starting point for creating classrooms and schools and programs that tap students' capacities is the deep belief of all staff that every youth is resilient. This means that every adult must grapple with questions like "What tapped my resilience? What occurred in my life that brought out my strength and capacity? How am I connecting this knowledge to what I do in the classroom or in this program?"

Resilience refers to persistence in achieving goals despite the obstacles life places in our way. Some children grow up with many obstacles across their paths; others have relatively smooth roads to travel. Either way, everyone encounters roadblocks sooner or later; the question is how someone surmounts them. Resilience involves

- willingness to take the road less traveled;
- willingness to overcome obstacles in trying to achieve goals;
- passion and purpose — going for your goals with drive, motivation, and personal involvement; and
- self-efficacy — belief in your ability to achieve the goals.

Schools can build students' resilience by modeling it, by implementing programs designed to develop it, and by creating challenging experiences for students that require resilience to see them through.

One way of developing resilience is to tell students about a challenging experience you have had in your own life, preferably when you were about the students' age, and how you got through the challenge.

What We Know about Student Achievement

- All students learn but not at the same pace.
- Students who are behind must work harder, longer and under better conditions.
- Students who are behind must be taught by effective teachers who care about them.
- Staff must understand how to work with students and parents from cultures different than their own.

You can then encourage students to share their own challenges and how they have coped with them. The class can discuss what constitutes better and worse coping mechanisms, and how people can decide to employ better ones. (In my own case, when I talk to students, I often tell them that I was the only kid of color in my class and how that was tough on me.)

Believing in students' resilience requires foremost that adults believe in their own innate capacity to transform and change. Our walk always speaks louder than our talk. So, to teach students about their internal power, adults must first see that they have the power — no matter what external stresses they face — to let go of conditioned thinking and access innate capacities for compassion, intuition, self-efficacy, and hope. Only when this belief is in place are adults truly able to create the connections and invite the contributions that will engage the innate resilience in students.

Many teachers do sincerely care about their students. But some, because of heavy teaching loads, feel overwhelmed by trying to meet the needs of so many students. Others may have a different set of priorities. To these teachers, "caring" may mean nothing more than providing students with the knowledge and skills needed for further education and for the workplace. Whatever the reason, the need to show personal concern for each student is not diminished. Ultimately, teachers' priorities determine what they do with their students.

The most successful efforts to keep at-risk students in school provide young people with a community of support that helps them feel connected to school and puts a value on learning. They also take advantage of student interests and strengths, and work to lessen the barriers that keep young people from participating. Teachers at these kinds of schools see educating at-risk students as a personal responsibility (Whelage et al. 1989).

Curriculum for the Whole Child

Research on early child development reveals the enormous plasticity of the human brain in the first years of life. In this period, brain tissue grows, the cerebral cortex is "wired," cognition develops, and speech as well as the capacity to manipulate language increases and matures. In short, many of the major tools that children employ in learning are well along in their development before they step through the school door. Many children enter school far in advance of their classmates, though. Research indicates, for example, that a child of college-educated parents begins Kindergarten with a working vocabulary of perhaps 20 000 words, compared with just 5000 for the children of high-school dropouts.

The old adage has it that "an ounce of prevention is worth a pound of cure." If schools are to succeed, they must address early childhood learning and development. More than that, they should be actively aligning their own Kindergarten activities with local preschool efforts so that schools are "ready" when the children arrive. The potential benefit is easy to define. Most children begin life equally equipped to learn and

What We Know about Students

- Many are bored and alienated in school.
- Much of what they know and how they learn is never recognized in school.
- The desire to learn must be cultivated.
- Less motivated students need support, encouragement, and regular feedback.
- Achievement may not reflect ability.
- High achievers must be pushed to think critically and creatively.
- Students must see how what they learn can help them to improve their lives.

— As identified by Pedro A. Noguera, Graduate School of Education, New York University grow. Preventing an achievement gap from developing is likely to be easier than fixing it after the fact.

To be engaging, curriculum and pedagogy must respond to the central qualities of children's development. A child must be treated as a whole person who has many needs — social, physical, aesthetic, ethical, and intellectual — and many ways to learn. Curriculum and pedagogy that emphasize a narrow range of cognitive skills and that have students sitting down with pencil and paper all day, giving them few opportunities to work collaboratively, will lose many children. In contrast, a curriculum rich in drama, music, art, mechanical and hands-on activity, and social interaction can engage a wide range of children — including those whose strong suit may not be paper-and-pencil seatwork.

Achievement improves with hands-on learning. Students who take part in active learning outperform their peers by 40 percent of a grade level in math and 70 percent of a grade level in science. Students whose teachers emphasize higher order thinking skills in math also outperform their peers by about 40 percent of a grade level (Wenglinsky 2000).

Similarly, what is known as "service learning" builds a sense of citizenship through involvement in civic action, increases students' sense of responsibility and workplace skills, and reduces negative behavior. One example of service learning is studying the health consequences of poor nutrition and lack of exercise and then organizing a health fair, creating a healthy food cookbook, and opening a fresh fruit and vegetable stand for the school and community (see Covitt 2002; Davila and Mora 2007; and Bradley 2005). A summary of studies on service learning found that students in elementary, middle, and high school made great academic strides through this educational approach. It fosters increased engagement in schoolwork, strengthens problem-solving skills, and contributes to improved attendance (Billig et al. 1999).

Engaging curriculum and pedagogy allows students to see the purpose of what they are learning. They solve problems that interest them and explore issues they find meaningful — sometimes because the problems and issues are "naturally" compelling, but often because teachers have taken pains to help children see how the lessons relate to what they want to know and do. Facts and skills are learned in the context of meaningful activities. For example, students learn to write by writing something that they wish to communicate, or they learn mathematics by using it to understand the world around them.

A culturally relevant classroom

An engaging pedagogy recognizes and fosters children's own efforts to make sense of the world. Much research demonstrates that children "construct" knowledge: that they are young scientists who continuously devise theories — physical, social, ethical — about how the world works and who accept or reject information about the world based on these powerful intuitive theories. Pedagogy, therefore, should use student culture in order to transcend the negative effects of the dominant culture on our young people, which come about, in part, through the failure of textbooks and curriculum to incorporate the history, culture, and background of the students to which they are directed.

Whose Culture Is Being Passed On?

Everyone who works (and studies) in our schools must consider these questions:

- Who creates knowledge?
- Who is empowered by it?
- How are different groups subordinated, marginalized, and excluded in education and culture?
- What are the possibilities for resistance?
- What are the possibilities for achieving a more just and equitable society through teaching (and learning)?

A culturally relevant classroom strives to focus on the goal of cultural excellence rather than cultural-deficit explanations. It challenges students by setting out expectations of their meeting high standards. It makes clear that effective instruction, above all else, is what the school is about. It assesses student knowledge regularly and thoroughly. And it recognizes the importance of building relationships with students.

A hallmark of cultural relevance is the notion that knowledge is something each student brings to the classroom. Students are not seen as empty vessels to be filled by all-knowing teachers. What they know is acknowledged, valued, and incorporated into the classroom. Students are given the right to question the curriculum, to think independently, to research, and to make their own sense of learning. And, as a matter of course, culturally relevant teaching makes a link between classroom experiences and the students' everyday lives.

In schools that show CARE, the curriculum engages the staff and students and prepares them for future challenges. Their vision of excellence in curriculum is to provide many educational opportunities that will enable students to reach their potential. A *rigorous* and *meaningful* curriculum

- is guided by specific, clearly stated, and challenging goals;
- allows students to understand what they are learning, why they are learning it, and when they have learned it;
- has a consistent scope and sequence aligned to standards between grades and subjects, with teachers understanding the relationship of their teaching to the rest of the curriculum; and
- is characterized by rich leadership and co-curricular and extracurricular opportunities that allow students to become well rounded and develop their unique talents and abilities.

A *quality* curriculum also has aspects that help students prepare for life beyond school:

- the integration of technology to engage students in their learning and provide them with the skills needed to accomplish their goals now and in the future;
- career/technical programs that are relevant to the needs of the twenty-first century and that result in appropriate industry credentials or program completion;
- career planning that fully prepares students to establish goals, choose appropriate courses to these ends, and make the transition to post-secondary education and/or careers; and
- work-based and/or experiential learning experiences integrated into all subjects that enhance the relevance of the curriculum to high school students.

Further, a *holistic* curriculum helps students become aware of their obligations as citizens in the midst of diversity by

- putting an emphasis on the development of a sense of social responsibility;

- promoting an awareness of and sensitivity to diversity in our community, so that students develop a sense of pride in their own heritage and respect for others;
- recognizing and nurturing all the different types of intelligences that students reveal; and
- fostering reflective skills so students are able to think critically, creatively, and positively.

A viable approach to educational instruction

In schools that show CARE, a vision of curriculum excellence goes hand in hand with a distinct approach to educational instruction. This approach is marked by several expectations:

- a school-wide expectation that in each classroom students will feel a sense of belonging, personal respect, and freedom (within agreed-upon) parameters to develop and express opinions, and become self-directed and self-analytical learners;
- high expectations for all students, regardless of gender, race, native language background, culture, or disability, demonstrated in scheduling practices, assignment of teachers, grading criteria, quality of work, and willingness of staff to provide extra time and help for students who need or want assistance;
- the expectation that teachers provide daily instruction that is engaging, rigorous, and relevant, using strategies that lead to proficiency and that hold students accountable for high-quality work; and
- the expectation that rubrics will clarify what students are to do and will define rigorous levels of high quality in classrooms.

This approach to educational instruction is based on certain common and research-based understandings:

- an understanding of the developmental characteristics of adolescents and how to address these in instructional strategies and classroom management;
- appropriate and pervasive use of research-based instructional strategies (e.g., identifying similarities and differences, summarizing and note taking, use of non-linguistic representations, cooperative learning, and generating and testing hypotheses, with the teacher acting as a facilitator of learning); and
- staff agreement on and enforcement of consistent school rules and procedures that help students gain skills and knowledge to succeed in their future roles in the community and workplace.

Educational instruction is also built on two commitments on the part of teachers across all subjects:

1. To develop twenty-first-century technological literacy in graduates and to give them the ability to share it with others; and

2. To enhance student vocabulary, the ability to write, and the ability to read with comprehension through use of content-appropriate strategies.

Quality of educational time

One key to curriculum excellence is the effective use of time. In schools that show CARE, the quality of educational time is the critical determinant of how much students will learn. When combined with effective school and classroom management as well as effective instruction, effective use of time is an important variable in student learning.

A good use of time in the learning process is tied to these principles:

- maximizing academic learning time within the school day through classroom time;
- using research-based instructional strategies to increase engaged learning time;
- finding creative and flexible ways of using time by providing school calendars and schedules to maximize the amount of quality learning time for all students;
- providing organizational options, such as more time at the early ages, extended hours in the junior grades, enrichment programs, and different age-level configurations that will allow students to master learning at their own pace and appropriate level of difficulty;
- creating flexible ways of providing professional development aimed at improving the effective use of class time and the quality of instruction; and
- facilitating effective use of time outside the school day that will enhance student learning opportunities.

Value of accessible health care

Of course, the best curriculum and instruction cannot benefit children who often miss school or who are sick or upset when they attend. When children receive regular health care, eat well, and know that they can find help with emotional and family concerns, they attend school more and can pay more attention to what they are learning. Students who use school-based health-clinic services use fewer drugs, have better school attendance and lower dropout rates, fail fewer courses, and have far fewer disciplinary referrals (Pearson, Jennings, and Norcross 1999).

Grades improve significantly when basic vision and hearing problems are corrected through accessible services. In one study, first- and second-graders suffering from vision problems were randomly assigned to control and treatment groups. Those receiving services had a 50 percent greater improvement rate than the control group in reading, almost a 100 percent greater improvement rate in math, and close to a 200 percent greater improvement rate in reading comprehension (Harris 2002).

Mental health services contribute to better school performance and an improved school climate, too. Students who receive such services have better attendance, fewer behavioral incidents, improved personal skills, better academic achievement, and a higher sense of school and home connectedness than students who do not (Center for Mental

Health in Schools 1999, 2000). Such services can promote students' self-confidence.

Positive impact of sports participation

Similarly, schools that offer intense physical activity programs see positive effects in academic achievement, including increased concentration; improved mathematics, reading, and writing test scores; and reduced disruptive behavior, even when time for physical education reduces the time for academics (Symons, Cinelli, Janes, and Groff 1997). As for organized sports activity in schools, it is widely recognized that sports may provide opportunities for character building and have a critical role in socializing youth.

As noted by Snyder and Spreitzer (1990), there are several reasons why participation in sport may enhance academic outcomes. Increased participation may lead to increased interest in school, including academic pursuits (the attraction of a college career in sports is often enough motivation for some athletes to strive for good grades); high academic achievement is valued in order to maintain eligibility to participate in sport (coaches constantly tell their student athletes, "No grades, no play"); increased self-confidence as a result of sports may spill over into academic performance; participation in sports often involves membership in groups with an orientation towards academic success (student athletes are aware that the road to professional sports goes through the university ranks, a recruiting ground for professional teams); and expectations of taking part in university sport may fuel the drive for academic excellence.

One outstanding example of the positive impact of sports on academic outcomes pertains to the Eastern Commerce Basketball Program. Since 2000–2001, the Toronto team has won five Ontario championships and played in seven of eight Ontario finals. Yet success in the classroom is the team's proudest accomplishment. A small inner-city school, Eastern Commerce has been a draw for youth following their hoop dreams for many years. Basketball players are held accountable both on and off the court. Player development focuses on academic, character, and skill development. Many special education and at-risk students have been able to transfer the discipline and structure experienced on the court into academic success. That success is manifest in the 98 percent graduation rate of basketball players who have completed their eligibility at the high school.

A caution about sports: Yet schools must keep the role of sports in perspective. Among Black youths, for example, the emphasis on sports has led athletes to become the top role models, which, in turn, may operate in concert with peer-group pressure to produce poor academic performance.

In any elementary school, close to 90 percent of all Black males want to become professional athletes. The problem is that, realistically, less than 1 percent will do so. When the rest realize this, they become a generation of could-have-beens. They have spent so much time preparing to be great athletes that their studies have likely suffered. On this matter, Joe Paterno, the head football coach at Penn State University, has said: "We have taken kids and sold them on a bouncing ball and running

See the teacher profile under "Teaching beyond the Classroom" in Chapter 6 of this book.

"I started to understand the direct correlation between life and basketball and why it was so important to be on time for practice, and being able to listen to what a coach is saying and execute what has been asked of you. Eastern Commerce probably saved my life."

— Dwayne Sybbliss, Eastern class of 2001
Ryerson University
Currently a Youth Worker at Covenant House, Toronto

"Roy Rana has been the mentor through the hard times on and off the court, my backbone throughout my high school basketball career. The respect I have grown to develop for him will never shatter as he has been loyally by my side through the tough and ugly of situations. His skills have molded the toughness and developed the man I am today."

— Tyrone Mattison, Eastern class of 2004
Graduate, Long Island University

"This program has had a significant impact on me because of all the great people I was surrounded by, people who cared and wanted what was best for me. Being surrounded by people in that context, they have instilled in me hard work, determination, and to always have a positive attitude. This has helped me to overcome the obstacles that I had to overcome which wasn't easy."

— Keaton Cole, Eastern class of 2008
Freshman, Western Carolina University

with a football and that being able to do certain things athletically was an end in its self. We cannot afford to do that to another generation."

The benefits of involvement in the arts

The arts engage all students in education, from those already considered successful and in need of greater challenges, to those who would otherwise remain disconnected and perhaps not realize their own potential for success. The arts encourage self-directed learning, helping to develop the capacity of students to strive for greater success. They provide a strong motivator for students to develop self-discipline and social skills.

The arts encourage other important aspects of learning, too. They provide an avenue for students to be able to express themselves and connect with their peers through personal growth and cooperative learning experiences. Expression in the arts helps students to develop cognitive and physical skills. The arts help students to make new connections, transcend previous limitations, and think "outside of the box." The arts give students the opportunity to represent what they have learned, thus achieving greater comprehension and retention of the material being covered.

The arts help to transform the school environment into an environment of discovery and learning. Strong, sequential arts education programs promote cultural literacy in our society. The arts are essential to an understanding of personal, local, national and global cultures, past and present. They break down barriers between disciplines and improve the conditions of learning. Each art form brings special ways of perceiving the world and mentally organizing and retrieving information, utilizing critical thinking and problem-solving skills. Education in the arts helps students to acquire skills that will be essential to their future success.

Students who are highly involved in the arts do better than those who are not. "And a growing amount of evidence shows that the arts can be particularly beneficial to students from economically disadvantaged backgrounds, and can even keep some potential dropouts in school" (Hicks 2004). One study found that low-income Grade 8 students highly involved in arts activities were more likely to score in the top two quartiles on standardized tests and less likely to be bored or drop out by Grade 10 (Catterall et al. 1998). Marybeth Gasman (2003) reported that in an analysis on 25 000 middle and high school students, it was found that students highly involved in the arts "performed better on a variety of academic measures than other students." The arts help to provide experiences for students to become lifelong learners after they reach adulthood, creating awareness that learning is a never-ending process.

Music instruction, in particular, appears to have special value. For certain learners, music can be a gateway to knowledge. And for all students, learning to play a musical instrument helps them to develop mentally, emotionally, and socially. It appears that music instruction enhances coordination, concentration, and memory, and improves eyesight and hearing (Muller 1993). More generally, it contributes to the school and community environment; provides an outlet for

Involvement in the arts leads to an acceleration of achievement because it promotes student engagement, focus, and pride. The arts connect to emotion, which is needed in order to integrate new information into memory. They flesh out ideas in many dimensions.

Project Art Smart

This program has enabled Hamilton-Wentworth students with an interest in the arts to sing, dance, play, and act while earning credits towards their diplomas. Exploring the tradition of musical theatre, it involves partnerships with local theatre groups. Students can take part in arts programming in drama, vocal and instrumental music, jazz, dance, musical theatre, technical theatre, and digital recording. Their talents are showcased in a final production seen by staff, other students, and community members.

self-expression and fosters creativity; strengthens feelings of self-worth; develops intelligence in other areas; and provides opportunities for success for students who have difficulty with other aspects of the school curriculum.

Common Assessment

Rick Stiggins (1997) writes that "assessment for learning means that assessments are used both to identify students who need additional support and to identify teacher practice. Teachers within a grade-team work together to build common assessments of essential learning. These assessments are timely, and give teachers and students frequent, ongoing feedback and answer the question: how do we know if each of our students is acquiring the knowledge and skills required?"

All schools that show CARE embrace this view of student assessment. For them, assessment is a balanced, seamless, and ongoing process that focuses on what students need to know and be able to do. The assessment system provides direction for continuous improvement, effective teaching and learning, and the establishment of a positive school environment. It also applies twenty-first-century, balanced standards throughout teaching and learning to diagnose student needs, plan next steps in instruction, and provide students with descriptive feedback they can use to improve the quality of their work. To achieve these objectives, the schools make wide use of performance-based assessments (e.g., projects, demonstrations, essays, debates, simulations, products) to evaluate higher order thinking skills and the ability to use and apply information; they also use grading and feedback practices that keep students well informed of their progress and build on their ability to demonstrate mastery of a skill or subject.

Teachers of the same course or grade level should have absolute common agreement on what they expect all their students to know and be able to do. Therefore, they should have common, collaboratively scored assessments at least once each quarter. The classroom activities leading up to those assessments may differ; the need to administer the same assessment should not. When assessment for learning is done well, it becomes a powerful strategy for improving student learning: teachers skilled at assessing can disaggregate and make student achievement a tool for realizing further improvement. One observer writes that "the combination of three concepts constitutes the foundation for results: meaningful teamwork; clear, measurable goals; and the regular collection and analysis of performance data. Good faith efforts to establish goals and then to collectively and regularly monitor and adjust actions toward them produce results and results goad, guide and motivate groups and individuals" (Schmoker 1999).

Giving the assessments is not so much what's important; what's important is doing something with the results.

This vision of common assessment, and its accompanying benefits, is summarized in Table 1 (on the next page).

Table 1 Common Assessment: Components and Benefits

Components	Benefits
An ongoing monitoring process for every student's learning, both formal and informal	*Efficiency:* by sharing the load, teachers save time
Bias-free assessments that are aligned with the articulated curriculum and instruction	*Fairness:* promotes common goals, similar pacing, and consistent standards for assessing student proficiency
Ongoing professional development of required skills in the design and administration of assessment, as well as evaluation of the quality of assessment methods	*Improved teacher practice:* provides teachers with a basis of comparison regarding the achievements of their students, so they can see the strengths and weaknesses of their teaching
Assessment of school climate and its effects on student performance	*Team capacity:* collaborative teacher teams are able to identify and address problem areas in their programs
Use of assessment results to evaluate programs and target areas for improvement	*Collective response:* helps teams and the school create timely, systematic interventions for students
Communication with and education of parents, students, and community about the need for accountability through the use of a varied and balanced assessment system	
Early identification of children with special learning needs and ongoing re-evaluation of all performance data	
Involvement of students in designing, using, and establishing criteria for assessment	
Creation of procedures for collecting and summarizing assessment information and for sharing it with the community, with special priority given to goals and objectives	

Building of Professional Learning Capacity

The purpose of professional development is to engage the staff in implementing effective instructional practices that improve the quality of learning and life for students. Professional development is an essential and indispensable process that embraces continuous improvement through providing thoughtfully designed learning opportunities.

If student achievement is to become the "main thing," a lot of work needs to be done to improve staff capacity. Specifically, all educators must make an ongoing effort to improve their own knowledge and skills as lifelong learners; to identify learning needs at the board, school, and individual levels, as well as effective research-based instructional practices; and to offer continuous support for new practices during implementation and for research studies dealing directly with classroom issues.

All of this can be accomplished if educators work together as a professional learning community (PLC). In schools that show CARE, educators accept learning as the fundamental purpose of their school and therefore are willing to examine all practices in light of their impact on learning. They are committed to working together to achieve their collective purpose. They cultivate a collaborative culture through the development of high-performance teams. And they assess their effectiveness on the basis of results rather than intentions. Individuals, teams, and schools seek relevant data and information and use that information to promote continuous improvement.

Dynamic collaboration

Collaboration is essential. By this, I mean a systematic process in which administrators, teachers, and support staff work together interdependently to analyze professional practice in order to improve our individual and collective results. Key features of this process are the following:

- Collaboration is embedded in routine practices.
- Time for collaboration is built into school days and the school calendar.
- Teams focus on key questions.
- Products of collaboration are made explicit.
- Team norms guide collaboration.
- Teams pursue specific and measurable performance goals.

Once a collaborative process along these lines is put in place, its success can be measured by addressing four questions. First, does it focus on the critical questions of learning? Second, does it lead to concrete changes in classroom practice? Third, does it increase the team's ability to achieve its goals? Fourth, does it help individual teachers, the team at large, and the school do a better job of helping all students learn at high levels? Professional learning communities shift the focus of their school improvement efforts from the supervision and evaluation of individual teachers to an emphasis on building the capacity of teams of teachers to take responsibility for their own learning.

Parental Involvement

A synthesis of 51 studies on parental involvement in education found that "student achievement increased directly with the extent to which parents were engaged in the program" (Henderson and Mapp 2002).

Parents' involvement in their children's education appears to have several other positive results, too. According to a study of 1200 New England urban students, when parents actively participate in their children's school and interact with their children's teachers, they gain a greater understanding of the expectations that schools have for students and learn how they can enhance their children's learning at home (Izzo et al. 1999). When parents are encouraged to help their children, they make good use of available social supports and place high priority on activities with their children (Cochran and Henderson 1986). The more involved parents are in their children's education, the more likely they are to continue their own education. They thereby serve as even more effective teaching resources and role models for their children (Henderson and Berla 1994).

Consistent parental involvement at home and at school — at every grade level and throughout the year — is important for students' sustained academic success and future aspirations. Students learn more and perform better when they receive consistent messages about the value and importance of education and support from parents, teachers, and churches (Sanders and Herting 2000). Families are best able to improve their children's life chances when they create a home environment that encourages learning, express high but realistic expectations for their children's achievement and future careers, and are involved in their children's school and community (Henderson and Berla 1994).

The quality of parent–teacher interactions can predict improvement both in children's behavior and in their academic achievement. Teachers tend to have higher expectations of those students whose parents collaborate with their schools, and children have higher test scores and grades when their parents are more involved (Larueau 1987). Students are more likely to bond with their teachers and learn from them when they see frequent, positive interaction between their family members and school staff (Comer 1988). And students whose parents stay closely involved in their educational progress throughout school are more likely to stay in school and to enter and finish college (Epstein 1992).

Parental involvement is a more accurate predictor of student achievement than family income or socio-economic status (Henderson and Berla 1994). When low-income parents are supported in child-rearing strategies, taught to interact with their children in learning activities at home, and encouraged to look to each other as resources, their children perform as well in preschool as middle-class children (Cochran and Henderson 1986). School-wide programs that work with parents to develop young people's behavioral, social, and academic capacity help increase academic and social skills and reduce behavioral referrals and suspensions (Comer and Haynes 1992).

As students get older, parental involvement shifts from school to home. When parents talk about school, encourage studying and learning, guide their children's academic decisions, support their aspirations,

The Parent Academy

Imagine a curriculum that equips parents with new skills, knowledge, and confidence to champion their children's education. The Parent Academy of Miami–Dade County Public Schools is a year-round initiative that provides parents with access to classes and courses offered in facilities all over that large school system. The campus encompasses schools, private businesses, public libraries, and online opportunities. Parents enroll in the classes that interest them most. Among these might be effective discipline, nutrition, financial management, and child development.

Inspired by this example, the Hamilton-Wentworth District School Board introduced Focus 4 Family, which offers free educational, recreational, and creative programs for families. The goal is to create engaging, empowering learning opportunities for all families within the board.

and help them plan for post-secondary education, their children are more likely to earn higher grades and test scores, enrol in higher level classes, and earn more course credits, regardless of family income and education (Catsambis and Garland 1997).

Considering all of this, schools need to acknowledge parents as their child's first teacher. Parental involvement in the education of their children should be encouraged to create a positive learning environment both at home and at school. Educators, parents, and students should work as a team to support all students in reaching their full potential, with families engaged in making decisions affecting their children's education and in expanding their repertoire as teachers, advocates, and partners. Schools should invite parents to take an active role in decision making at the school level, encourage honest communication about difficult issues, and create relationships that share power and responsibility (Sanders and Herting 2000). Supporting school councils and Parent Involvement Committees are two strong ways.

As for parents, their responsibility is manifold. They should make education a priority, participate in out-of-school educational experiences, communicate with their children about school, and provide a positive, nurturing, and caring home environment for optimal growth and learning. They should support education by emphasizing the value of lifelong learning. And they should participate in discussions and decision-making processes that affect children, families, and the quality of schooling.

Parents play a vital role in the development and education of their children and in the success of schools. They are the most important influence in a child's life outside of school. Long after direct learning from parents in a child's early years gives way to formal education, parents continue to play a key role in student success through the attitudes they help to shape and the direct supports they provide.

Research clearly indicates that good schools become better schools when there is a strong connection with parents as part of the learning community. The positive results of a genuine partnership between parents and schools include improved student achievement, reduced absenteeism, better behavior, and restored confidence among parents in their children's schooling.

School councils have a unique role to play in bringing parents and schools together as partners. They provide an important bridge between school staff, parents, community members, Home and School Associations, and other parent groups that may be active within the school community.

Engagement of the Broader Community

Parental involvement in education is part and parcel of a much larger project — community engagement. Research shows a positive association between school, family, and community partnerships and beneficial outcomes of such relationships for students, parents, and teachers (Eccles and Harold 1993). Communities should be encouraged to become increasingly involved with and committed to improving our

In Ontario, for example, the ministry of education has a mandate to enhance parental involvement in education. Under a policy released in 2005, the Parent Involvement Committee (PIC) works to engage parents by providing support and resources to encourage their participation in their children's personal and academic success. School councils work with their schools and the PIC to identify project opportunities to increase parental engagement. Schools and their school councils may apply for special funds and grants to aid the development of creative projects.

Overall, research indicates that parental involvement at home has more impact on student achievement than parental involvement in school-based activities (see Jeynes 2005).

While research proves that students benefit directly when their parents are involved in their education, parents enjoy benefits, too: they learn more about public education, become part of a school community, and become engaged as citizens (see Corter and Pelletier 2004).

schools. Members can make a difference in students' lives by spending quality time helping them grow into successful adults and serving as tutors and mentors. Other community engagement opportunities can also be pursued. For example, businesses and community organizations can offer services and support to a school to benefit student achievement programs, participation in school assemblies, school beautification, and other student enrichment activities. As we strive to foster greater achievement for children, our schools should welcome community agencies, organizations, businesses, and individuals to provide valued input.

Yet, despite the widely acknowledged benefits of parental and community involvement in education, many schools still have limited relationships with their students' families and communities. In schools that show CARE, by contrast, the school community recognizes the importance of effective communication and productive working relationships with the local community (parents, residents, senior citizens, businesses, government agencies, and civic, religious, cultural, and volunteer groups). More will be said on this in the next chapter, which, in the context of a larger discussion of the importance of school climate, addresses the matter of "community schools." Here, it is sufficient to note that the community relationships at the heart of schools that show CARE encompass a unified plan that develops a sense of ownership and pride in all aspects of the community.

Listen, inform, and encourage

Communication is one indicator of schools that show CARE — and listening is a big part of that. The public is desperate to put their ideas and concerns before educational leaders. People urgently want us to listen to what they think. Sometimes, they don't expect us to do anything about it, but they *do* expect us to listen. Listen, listen, listen — this is good advice for educational leaders. So too is communicate, communicate, communicate.

Community engagement is not a process of persuading local citizens that the school or board is right; it is a process of helping them come to public judgment about the issues facing the school or board. In the end, taking the time to do this means that the public is more likely to support school or board initiatives. If you expect people to share your agenda, let them in on the takeoffs as well as the landings.

Community involvement depends on effective *two-way* communication. Educational leaders can provide information and seek feedback from the community, along with opportunities to support and reinforce the value of learning for all students by demonstrating the relevance of learning beyond the walls of the school. To this end, they should encourage members of the community to attend events, volunteer, and contribute to programs and processes designed to enhance school life. By reinforcing the value of citizenship and community service, community involvement in education will foster positive relationships — both within the community and beyond — while underlining the accountability of the school and the community in meeting their mutual goal of preparing students to be productive citizens and lifelong learners.

The role of a board of education is not to run schools, but to see that they are well run. Elected trustees serve as policy makers, providing direction, a basis for decision making, and an imperative for action. They need to be aware of the concerns of parents, students, board staff, unions, and community organizations. They play a key role in engaging the community, listening, managing expectations, communicating goals and progress, and celebrating successes.

CHAPTER 3

School Climate

R esearch has established that "motivation and learning increase when young people spend time in safe settings that offer structured enrichment activities and acknowledge their need for control, choice, competence and belonging" (Blum, Beuhring, and Rinehart 2000). Schools that show CARE recognize this reality. Staff, students, and parents care for, respect, and trust one another. There is a common purpose and shared sense of belonging, cohesiveness, and pride in the school. Morale is high. Social and academic growth are continuous.

Vision for a Safe, Responsive Climate

This vision for a school climate encompasses many aspects, several of which are outlined below.

The school climate is characterized by a sense of caring:

- In this atmosphere, feelings, concerns, and conflicts receive fair and consistent attention.
- A caring ethic promotes compassion, kindness, respect for differences, and a genuine interest in each other.
- A welcoming environment allows parents and teachers to work cooperatively for student and school progress.

With such a school climate, there is a vibrant learning community:

- There is a genuine mutual respect and a high level of trust.
- The learning community has a common mission and purpose.
- Members feel a sense of pride in the school building.
- Commitment is made to providing opportunities for the development of teacher-leaders and for the acknowledgment and celebration of special contributions and achievements of others.
- Learning is celebrated through attractive displays of quality student work.

A sense of responsibility pervades the climate.

- Staff members are aware of the importance of being positive role models.

"Inclusion is not bringing people into what already exists; it is making a new space, a better space for everyone."

— George Dei

- Responsible citizenship, which includes student leadership activities and student achievement, is emphasized.
- Everyone upholds the belief that all children will learn and are committed to ensuring their success.

Benefits of fostering respect and trust

Everyone in the school should be treated with the same respect, courtesy, and friendliness accorded to the most influential people. Schools that show CARE insist on respect. In a complex changing society, building respect among people from different backgrounds is a never-ending school responsibility, something that must be actively fostered by staff and community alike.

Schools that show CARE are much more likely to have higher student achievement than schools with poor relationships. Researchers analyzed 100 schools that had large gains in standardized math and reading tests over five years and 100 schools that did not make much improvement. One out of two schools that had high trust levels between staff and parents made significant improvements; only one out of seven schools with low trust levels made such gains. The schools that had a low trust level and improved anyway were those that built and strengthened trust over a five-year period; schools that remained without a trusting community made no academic gains (Bryk and Schneider 2002). Positive relationships between staff and parents are essential.

Lead to Succeed

In schools that show CARE, leadership embraces shared decision making, positive support, a culture of inquiry, and an ethic of caring. Shared leadership enables all members of the learning community to become skilled participants and strategic leaders. This leadership emerges as individuals learn together and orchestrate constructive change towards realizing a shared vision.

Effective leaders, who may be found anywhere in the organizational structure, are committed to keeping the dream of educational excellence alive, and that objective entails the adoption of key values. These leaders believe that the school's vision has to be a collective one, crafted collaboratively, with generosity of spirit. They know that the dream must be student centred, focused on ambitious academic goals, and continuously evolving. They also know that realizing the dream hinges partly on operating consistently according to values and beliefs tied to that vision. In different ways, they ask themselves daily: *Does this decision help realize the dream?*

The actions of effective leaders are based on a well-formed set of values, beliefs, and understandings. Committed to a moral purpose and vision, such leaders can achieve a community consensus on school goals and priorities. They have the strength of character to persevere with this purpose or the vision to change practices in the light of evolving understandings. They also understand the nature of power and change, and know that the quality of their relationships with students, staff,

"Inclusive education is central to the achievement of high quality education for all learners and the development of more inclusive societies. Inclusion is still thought of in some countries as an approach to serving children with disabilities within general educational settings. Internationally, however, it is increasingly seen more broadly as a reform that supports and welcomes diversity amongst all learners."

— UNESCO, *Inclusive Education*

"The old adage 'People are your most important asset' turns out to be wrong. People are not your most important asset. The right people are."

—Jim Collins, *Good to Great*

Lessons from Peter Drucker about Leadership

1. A leader is someone who has followers.
2. Popularity is not leadership — results are.
3. Leaders are highly visible; they set examples.
4. Leadership is not rank, privilege, titles or money — it is responsibility.
5. Leaders lift others.
6. Leaders value their teams.

— Identified by John C. Maxwell, *Five Habits of Effective Executives* and community is crucial to their ability to enable others to learn. Accordingly, they promote an atmosphere of care and trust within the school community, setting the tone for mutually respectful relationships. This trust grows by providing individual moral support, taking account of people's opinions, and appreciating their work.

Effective leaders are learners and they know how to support and challenge the learning of others. They understand learning and teaching. They focus on the improvement of student outcomes and the building of learning communities; they have high expectations for students and teachers. Leaders facilitate opportunities for staff to learn from each other and provide a model of continuous learning by viewing all experiences as learning experiences.

Effective leaders contribute to collective professional knowledge through a research- and theory-based practice. They integrate their leadership and management roles by focusing on the improvement of student outcomes that are supported by organizational structures and processes. They redesign school structures to promote participatory decision making. They advocate staff professionalism and promote it through professional networks and alliances beyond the school.

Successful instructional leadership focuses on the continuous improvement of student outcomes, develops learning communities that engage the wider community, and builds leadership capacity as well as social and intellectual capital. This kind of leadership requires a deep understanding of quality teaching and learning, and a strong commitment to shared educational and social values. School leaders have the ultimate responsibility of redesigning schools to fulfill the learning needs of all students. Research on schools where students have made great gains in learning shows that moral leadership and high expectations are key.

Transformational leadership

Effective leaders put instruction at the top of the agenda. While the managerial and political dimensions of the job will not go away, these roles should be aligned with the overriding goal of improving instruction. Transforming schools into learning organizations requires moving beyond implementing best practices in professional development to re-culturing our sites. It means shifting the work of staff from service delivery to professional learning. Schools as learning organizations are defined by their focus on student outcomes, use of data to inform decision making, ability to create productive collaborative structures, development of a common vision, curricular coherence, and targeted professional development.

System-wide transformation means that the root causes of problems are squarely addressed and then solved. That requires senior education leaders to take new approaches to address the systemic issues:

- to act on the basis of personal courage, passion, and vision, not on the basis of fear, self-survival, or self-interest; and
- to conceive of their districts as whole systems, not as a confederation of individual schools and programs.

It also requires leaders and followers

- who are willing and able to break or circumvent rules to create paradigm change, not bound by rules;
- who have a clear view of the opportunities that systemic transformation offers them, not the view "We can't do this because . . . "; and
- who possess the professional intellect, change-minded attitudes, and change navigation skills to create transformational change in their districts, not people without an inkling about how to navigate such change.

Finally, it requires the human, technical, and financial resources to sustain a transformation journey over five to seven years — large-scale change can take this long — not resources "stolen" from successful programs to pay for transformational change.

Transformational education leaders who show CARE, then, will do the following:

1. Facilitate the development, articulation, and implementation of a shared vision of learning, and act as positive role models for the children and the community.
2. Understand the dynamics of change and facilitate meaningful change based upon knowledge of best practices that ensure student achievement.
3. Advocate and sustain an educational culture conducive to student learning and staff professional growth.
4. Facilitate the establishment of a curriculum framework that provides direction for teaching and learning and is aligned with the school's mission as well as government standards.
5. Improve the schools' programs and services by using assessments that are based on data analysis and involve input from, and are reported to, various stakeholders.
6. Recognize a variety of ideas, values, and cultures, as well as the importance of diversity, and support effective school improvement efforts with enthusiasm and energy.

Working towards equitable schools

Finally, in order to create equitable schools — and I do think that is the end game for all of us — we, as leaders, must be the guardians of equity. We cannot begin to talk about the opportunity to learn without discussing how resources — money, time, personnel, facilities, materials, academic and other supports, and more — are distributed to ensure that no matter where students are, they receive the resources they require to support their expected success and excellence in school performance.

To me, culturally proficient leadership is an approach for closing the achievement gaps created by differences in resources. It involves seeing the differences in resources and responding positively, adapting and differentiating to the needs of the learners. It then examines the values and behaviors of an individual person or school and the policies and

"The significant new investments in education are not reaching many of the children who need most help because long identified barriers to learning are not being addressed."

— Roy McMurtry and Alvin Curling, *Review of the Roots of Youth Violence* practices of schools and systems that enable the person or the school to interact effectively in a culturally diverse environment.

How to Improve Students' Quality of Life

The Role of Leaders in School Improvement Efforts

- To provide the vision — to keep the big picture clear (Why are we doing this? What will we achieve?)
- To make it possible for staff to have time to meet and plan: to develop "buy-in"
- To keep things moving, but try not to impose decisions
- To work with staff and parents to develop a clear mission and clear priorities
- To provide support in areas where help is needed

Effective leaders cultivate a broad definition of *community* and consider the contribution that every member can make to helping children achieve their full potential. They hear the voices of many stakeholders — families, businesses, and other groups and institutions. Their ability to develop plans that reflect the legitimate influence of others draws in many partners, whose personal passions as well as community spirit foster participation. They look for evidence of widespread participation in important aspects of change. Establishing partnerships and listening to a chorus of voices are leadership skills that permeate all aspects of their work.

The process of encouraging people to take more action at the local level is known as "community development." It rests upon the assumption that the best way (and often the only good way) for improvement to come about is to start at the grass roots. People work together in their community to name injustices and struggles, understand where they come from, and take action to make positive changes. There is a strong belief in "empowerment," aimed directly at the individual and at the local community. The more people involved in making decisions and taking action, the better it is.

Community development has two basic goals: first, to improve the quality of life of all community members, and, second, to involve all community members in the process. It is believed that these goals can best be accomplished by raising the knowledge level of all community members through better education for both youth and adults.

Collectively, individual teachers and schools can make a significant difference in the lives of students, and in the quality of community life, by helping them become responsible, caring people. Doing so requires making an ethic of caring a central part of a school's program. An *ethic of caring* is defined as "acts done out of love and natural inclination" (Noddings 1988, 1), with the goal of helping all students "grow and actualize" themselves (Mayeroff 1977, 1). Two interrelated factors are essential for its development:

- schools that, as a whole, are caring communities; and
- individual teachers who care.

In schools that exemplify an ethic of caring, values, such as self-respect and cooperation, are incorporated into the learning process and encourage students to develop self-understanding as well as insights into others. Caring values are about developing skills to handle emotions and understand how emotional responses can affect others. Positive self-worth is critical to a child's development and will help develop a respect for others in the community. Being responsible for something or someone helps students develop an understanding of personal accountability and the consequences of their behavior and actions; it challenges them to uphold their personal values. Fostering a culture of cooperation means working for the good of all, focusing on the whole. Caring promotes values such as compassion, empathy, sharing, friendship, trust, and self-esteem.

At the core of the learning process is emotional intelligence. A safe, happy, and vibrant learning environment offers strong support and professional guidance to students. Able to think critically and creatively, they understand why developing meaningful relationships is important and they value caring for other people and the world around them. They may also develop positive and productive dispositions to learning, and become resilient and empowered — ready to meet challenges along the way.

Resilience is crucial to life success. It is important that students learn how to persevere after a setback. They need to have the confidence to assess a situation critically and move forward in the face of adversity. Having positive self-regard helps them to realize their dreams, strive for their maximum potential, and work at their highest level.

Given the importance of promoting students' self-regard, educators need to reflect on how they interact with their students. They need to ask questions such as these:

- How well do I know my students?
- What do I know about their likes and dislikes, interests and goals, or special talents?
- How often do I compliment individual students for work well done?
- How much time do I spend one on one with each student?
- When I do spend time with individual students, is it primarily disciplinary or is it a positive experience?
- Does my interest in each student extend beyond the classroom to his or her out-of-school activities?
- How often do I communicate with parents in sharing positive things about their child's progress or in seeking their help in making school a more positive experience for their child?

Educators' answers to these and similar questions may be useful in helping them focus on how best to serve and support students.

A Sense of Belonging

"There is an increasing body of knowledge showing that students who feel connected to school — to teachers, to other students, and to school itself — do better academically."

— Franklin P. Schargel, Tony Thacker, and John S. Bell, *From At Risk to Academic Excellence*

Today's culture lacks places for people to belong and has substituted material wealth for interpersonal richness; however, a school that shows CARE creates a learning community that invites a sense of belonging.

There are many ideas about the significance of a sense of belonging. A few researchers define it as the extent to which students feel personally accepted, respected, included, and supported in the school social environment (Goodenow and Grady 1993). Maslow (1962) argues that the need of belonging has to be satisfied before other needs can be met. In the identification-participation model, students must identify well

The Three Cs of Belonging

Connect: Students connect through cooperative learning and teacher encouragement.
Capable: Teachers promote this sense in students.
Contribute: Students do volunteer work that makes them feel valued.

with their schools — feel welcomed, respected, and valued — or their educational participation will be limited (Finn 1989). Applying the principles of affective psychology, another researcher states that successful student learning depends, in part, on the feeling of belonging or of being cared for (Combs 1982).

Students who feel connected to their school and to the people at their school report higher levels of emotional well-being. The bond they feel with the school serves as a protective shield against unhealthy behaviors and decisions, such as using alcohol and illegal drugs, engaging in violent or abnormal behavior, becoming pregnant, and experiencing emotional distress (McNeely, Nonnemaker, and Blum 2002). In a review of empirical studies on the growth and nature of juvenile gangs, Burnett and Walz (1994) conclude that gang-related problems increase when students lack a sense of belonging to their school.

The sense of belonging has been conceptualized as three Cs: connect, capable, and contribute (Xin Ma 2003). The first C emphasizes that students need to connect with one another by cooperative learning and with teachers by receiving encouragement from them. The second C emphasizes that teachers need to help students feel capable (for example, by modifying tasks and assignments to provide students with successful learning experiences). The third C emphasizes that students need to contribute to their school by performing duties that make them feel valued (for example, by being lunch monitors).

Teachers also benefit from feeling connected to a positive school community. Teaching effectiveness and teacher satisfaction are related to the extent to which teachers view their work environment as a community — one that encourages collaboration and teacher involvement in school decision making and shared goals (Lee, Dedrick, and Smith 1991). Teachers who see themselves as full and active members of the school community "create similar learning contexts for their students" (Becker and Riel 1999). School administrators should ensure that teachers feel a sense of belonging to school so that they, in turn, can help their students feel this sense.

Schools That Show CARE — Community Schools

Schools that show CARE are, by definition, community schools. In general terms, this means that the partners who share their assets and expertise with such schools are important sources of "social capital." Just as financial capital — money — enables people to purchase goods and services, social capital connects them to people and information that can help them solve problems and meet their goals.

For people of all ages, social capital makes it easier to share expertise, succeed individually, and contribute to a healthy community. For young people, in particular, social capital increases exposure to role models and life options. It enhances their sense of connectedness to others, their sense of security, and their belief in the future. For many of them, especially those from less affluent communities and lower income families, however, social capital — like financial capital — is not readily available.

The building of social capital

Schools that show CARE consciously work to change this. By serving as community schools, they build social capital through, for example, mentoring relationships with caring adults. School-to-work learning experiences significantly increase young people's knowledge of career choices and help them develop the skills needed to pursue them. When young people have such experiences, they create important relationships with supportive, caring adults. They also learn new ways of acquiring and using knowledge through exposure to challenging and engaging experiences, and benefit from opportunities for meaningful involvement. They are more likely to become economically self-sufficient, healthy, and productive family members and citizens than those who do not have these experiences (Connell, Gambone, and Smith 2000).

The integration of quality education with services

The community schools movement is part of a growing revolution against a fragmented approach to the challenges presented by children seen as at-risk. A community school integrates the delivery of quality education with whatever health and social services are required in that community. These institutions draw on both school resources and outside community agencies that come into the schools and join forces to provide seamless programs (Dryfoos 1998, 73).

The U.S.-based Coalition for Community Schools identifies five areas for program and service development in community schools:

1. Quality educational services
2. Youth-development programs
3. Family-support activities
4. Family and community engagement
5. Community development

The full-service community school integrates services for families under one roof. This approach supports the teaching and learning mission of the school, while making services such as health screening, mental health, recreation, after-school programs, group counselling, cultural events, parent education, and welfare readily available for families. It is consistent with the wraparound model, where services are fitted to the needs of children rather than children fitted into programs.

Six traits characterize what Shaw and Replogle (1996, 9) term as "school-linked services":

- A holistic approach to children. Holism means that the relationship between health, familial adjustment and emotional well-being and learning is recognized. Programs are set up such that all factors supporting learning are addressed in a non-fragmented manner.
- Joint planning. To enjoy status as a full-service school, school officials, parents and community personnel must plan together for the well-being of children and families. It is essential that the views of parents be elicited and considered in decision making.

- Shared service delivery. In full-service schools, social services are either co-located or integrated with the administration.
- Collaboration and/or coordination. To be truly effective, schools, social service agencies and health providers must move beyond joint planning to, if not directly sharing resources, cooperating in their delivery. In the future, this may extend to joint use of facilities.
- Focus on child outcomes. Assessment of full-service school programs is predicated on measures of the well-being and achievement of students, rather than merely on "procedural compliance with rules and regulations."
- Shifts in professional roles. True collaboration requires eliminating professional turf battles in the interest of children. Educators, social workers, counsellors and health professionals will ultimately learn from one another as they serve youngsters. This blending of professional roles does not imply a complete merger, such as recasting teachers as mental-health providers.

Inventive, enduring partnerships

Using public schools as hubs, community schools knit together inventive, enduring relationships among educators, families, volunteers, and community partners. Families, youth, and residents join with educators and community partners to articulate shared goals for students and to help design, implement, and evaluate activities. Participation of these stakeholders as decision makers helps ensure that community schools meet local needs and show measurable progress.

These partnerships are organized around two common goals: (1) helping students learn and succeed, and (2) strengthening families and communities (Blank, Melaville, and Shaw 2003). By sharing expertise and resources, schools and communities act in concert to transform traditional schools into permanent partnerships for excellence. Schools value the resources and involvement of community partners, and communities understand that strong schools are at the heart of strong neighborhoods. Health and social service agencies, family-support groups, youth-development organizations, institutions of higher education, community organizations, businesses, and civic and faith-based groups all play a part.

In an increasingly complex and demanding educational climate, schools are not left to work alone.

Community schools promote both youth and adult development. They provide leadership-training programs and offer ongoing opportunities to students to hold decision-making roles, to speak out in school and community forums, and to work with others on school and community projects. Parents and community residents support their children's learning while developing their own knowledge and skills. Literacy classes, adult and parent education, employment training, family support, and leadership development all are part of the community school vision.

Community schools recognize that students who are physically, socially, and emotionally competent tend to succeed academically. Autonomy, awareness of others, responsibility, and rational optimism all inform academic achievement. In traditional schools, students who lack these essential, non-academic skills are, for the most part, left to acquire them outside school. That is not the case in community schools, however, where students have abundant opportunities for learning and exploration in school, after school, and in the community.

The linking of school and community gives community schools other distinct advantages over traditional schools, too. First, it garners additional resources and reduces non-instructional demands on school staff. By providing services and supports that address various needs of students, partnerships with the community enable educators to concentrate on curriculum and instruction. Second, drawing on community resources provides learning opportunities that enhance young people's social, emotional, and physical development as well as academic skills. Finally, community partnerships connect young people and their families to positive role models and make them more aware of life options. They offer students a source of social capital — the networks and relationships that create a sense of belonging and communicate the importance of education and belief in the future (Blank, Melaville, and Shah 2003).

Community school students show significant and widely evident gains in essential areas of non-academic development, too. As documented in *Making the Difference: Research and Practice in Community Schools* (Blank et al. 2003), they benefit from stronger parent–teacher relationships, increased teacher satisfaction, a more positive school environment, greater community support, and better use of school buildings. Partly as a result of the last point, the neighborhoods of community schools enjoy increased security, heightened community pride, and better rapport among students and residents.

Other research underscores the connections among school, home, family, community, and student achievement. Barton (2003) identifies 14 factors that correlate with student achievement. Six of these relate to the school environment, such as school curriculum, teacher preparation, and school safety. The remaining eight factors speak to the importance of family and community to student success; among them are parent availability and support, student mobility, television watching, and parental involvement. Barton concludes that "the education system cannot succeed in greatly reducing the gaps by going it alone" (37).

Open access schools

In community schools, children engage in creative educational projects and cultural enrichment from early in the morning until evening and all summer long. Examples of school-wide service projects include sponsoring a Seniors Day, undertaking a beautification project, sponsoring a luncheon for new students, organizing noontime intramural sports, and providing a luncheon for volunteer parents. Parents are welcome.

Children also take active part in community service. Projects might include organizing canned food drives; adopting a family during the holiday season; visiting a senior citizens' centre; helping with Special Olympics; taking part in a community cleanup day; volunteering at local elementary schools, daycare centres, or nursery schools; offering child care to parents attending school functions; planning a blood drive; and offering computer training.

Community schools fall on a continuum: some have one-item add-ons, such as after-school enrichment programs, while others constitute a fully realized and comprehensive alternative model. Almost all are built on partnerships between the school and such groups as community services, universities, businesses, churches, libraries, museums, the police, and youth agencies. All extend the school hours and all are child centred.

Community leaders and parents at the local level are enthusiastic about such schools — they *want* their school buildings open as much as possible. Keeping schools open longer before and after school, and during the summer, can turn them into community learning hubs. By leaving school doors open during non-traditional school hours, the school provides students, parents, and the community with access to valuable educational resources. The community school can be a safe after-school and summer haven for children, where learning takes place in a building removed from the violence, drugs, and lack of supervision that permeate some communities.

Schools as hubs in the community can serve as a critical resource to meet the growing need for children to have safe and productive activities during the hours outside the school day. Before- and after-school and summer programs help children stay on the right track from the beginning: these programs can provide reading tutors to younger children, mentors to guide older children, and so on. Working parents, too, want more access to extended learning opportunities.

See Chapter 5 for information on the teacher-generated Woodhill Summer Reading Program.

Public schools are uniquely suited to meet these formidable challenges. They provide low-cost, accessible locations to extend learning. They can offer children and youth long-term mentoring to help them master basic skills; at the same time, they can provide enrichment activities that often have the potential to develop into lifelong interests. They allow all partners in a child's education to become involved and utilize their diverse talents and resources; for example, science professionals can act as mentors and, in so doing, both share their expertise and serve as role models for the importance of education. Extending the hours that schools are open is a cost-effective means of allowing students to learn and develop in an enriching, safe, and drug-free environment.

How the School Needs to Work with the Community

In attempts to open schools to the outside world, a great deal of energy has been wasted through a lack of consensus. Staff, students, trustees, and community have to share a common interest in developing a community school. Even if all these players are highly motivated, they can quickly lose their staying power when it seems that a community school merely means more work, when increased commitment is not connected with incentives and results, and when financial, structural, and personnel support are not forthcoming.

The success of community use of a school is dependent on the school working with the community to fulfill the following:

- Integrate school and adult education. School classes and adult education should both take place on community school premises, functioning together with regard to content and context. Adults should be welcomed as students in the morning classes as well. In the afternoons and evenings, age-specific and mixed-age activities and courses should be offered.

- Put its available resources (e.g., workshops, specialty rooms, sports facilities, classrooms, kitchen, and library) at the disposal of its new clientele. The physical school has multiple functions, and not only on weekends.
- Make the school not only a learning venue, but also a cultural and leisure-time facility for community groups.
- Become a base for self-help for neighbors as well as unemployed youths, for people who wish to qualify themselves and upgrade their skills.
- Network with other external learning venues, and work on projects with other non-school groups and institutions.
- Build a sense of belonging, of community, thereby counteracting and reducing the alienation that so many young people feel at school.
- Make significant contributions to social development by promoting good neighborly relations and self-reliance.

Further criteria for a community school are set out below:

- A community school will need the leadership and management capacity to ensure that no additional burden is put on teachers. It will also need to be able to operate its programs without being distracted from its education agenda.
- School facilities will need to be open outside school hours, including weekends and holidays.
- All groups, including students, families, and the local community, should have access to a range of services and facilities at the school.
- Provision of activities and services should not have a negative impact on the main duty of the school — that is, to educate its students.
- A community school is expected to cooperate with board and provincial/state evaluation of its programs, activities, and standards.
- A community school must ensure that it has consulted with other board schools and the local community, and that demand exists for the core services it intends to offer.
- When developing proposals, a community school should keep in mind how those proposals will build positive links between people from different backgrounds within the community.
- All services should be accessible to as many local community groups as possible, taking account of relevant legislation and regulations — a community school should be welcoming, open, and accessible to all users.

Prime example of a community school: The Wever Community Hub

According to Principal Lori Kyle, before the hub's development, the inner-city community that the hub serves was characterized by high poverty, high crime, high unemployment, and low community engagement. The Cathy Wever Elementary School had a culture of hopelessness, anger, aggression, and deprivation. Participation in the Norman Pinky Lewis Recreation Centre programs was low because many families could not afford the fees. Even if money was not a barrier to participation, the violence, illegal drug use, sex-trade workers, and gang activity right outside the recreation centre deterred participation.

The problems were far outside the influence of the school, community recreation centre, or police alone, so community members decided to work together. The group believed that schools and recreation centres must be places where children and youth feel safe, secure, and at ease, and that it is the job of everyone in the community to ensure this. The Wever Community Hub has accessed financial support through a wide range of successful grant opportunities, but as important as funding is the work of passionate volunteers and community outreach personnel.

The group first created an after-school program that has been the hallmark of success. Bingo to Better Health was developed to remove all barriers to school-aged children for participation in free structured, supervised activities every day for two hours after school dismissal. Program participants receive a Bingo card with each square representing an activity. They take part in a variety of different activities in order to complete a number of lines or a full card. Activities include swimming, hip-hop dance, computer training, arts and crafts, and résumé writing. Between 100 and 120 students take part daily.

Since the initial success of the after-school program, grants have been plentiful. Funders, who are able to see the benefits to the community, are willing to fund support personnel for community outreach and administrative personnel to assist with fund-raising and grant writing as well as research and data collection.

The Wever Hub has expanded its programs. It now has a Mother's Cooking on a Budget class where parents learn how to prepare healthy food options for their family. An adult sewing club has allowed families to make their own pyjamas and tee shirts with fabric donated to the community. Women in a jewellery-making group have honed their skills and are now taking orders, something that has led to improved self-confidence and gain in entrepreneurial skills. At a nominal fee, families can now take their children to the "movies" one night per month and mingle with other families. A youth advisory group, as well as activities for seniors, is emerging.

The hub has brought many positive outcomes to its inner-city block. Drug use, gang activity, and violent crime have sharply declined. Attendance at the recreation centre has reached levels never before seen and among the highest recorded in the city. School data shows a marked and steady decline in office referrals and suspensions as well as an observable positive and respectful culture. A buzz of volunteer activity is evident in the school every day, including at the end when numerous teachers share programs of interest, and even on Saturdays and Sundays when free basketball is offered.

The Wever Hub has changed the culture of this community from hopelessness and danger to one of hope, health, and companionship. Community members of all ages now attend activities both at the recreation centre and school knowing that both environments are barrier free, safe, inviting, and inclusive. Former program participants are now employees of the hub, serving as positive role models and developing leadership skills that will take them into the world of work. Families who have little to give are giving back to their community through volunteerism. Children and families, now with a strong sense of belonging and pride in their community, are taking an active role in its development, ensuring that it will continue to thrive and improve.

The making available of health and social services

Beyond offering lifelong-learning programs, a community school could make available health and social services: health promotion and education; special education activities; teenage advice centres; drug-prevention and early intervention/treatment services; preventive health services, such as immunization; nutrition/obesity-related services and support; mental health services; parenting classes; and family support.

Each of the following programs and services that could be part of a community school must meet certain conditions. For all of them identified below, it is important that they be available throughout the calendar year and characterized by a wide range.

Lifelong learning: Open to all the community; wide range of programs covering many levels and abilities; qualification- and non-qualification-based programs;
Childcare: Open longer hours (e.g., 8 a.m.–6 p.m.); open for use by school staff and all local families, not just those with students at the school, and by all family members, not just parents;
Health and social services: Open to some or all students in the school, including students with special educational needs and disabilities and, wherever appropriate, students from other schools, families, and the local community;
Family learning: Open to all local families, not just those with students at the school, and all family members, not just parents;
Parenting support: Open to all local families, not just those with students at the school and all family members, not just parents;
Study support: Wide range of study-support and holiday activities;
Sports and arts: Wide range of sports and arts activities; open to all members of the community, including local sports clubs;
Information technology: Available for at least 10 hours per week; open to all members of the community.

Finally, a community school must take into account the extra costs associated with this type of education and extended building use. Specifically, there are the costs of staff to plan, develop, and operate the extended services, including the management of relationships between different agencies and the raising of funds from other sources; of extra caretaking or volunteers' expenses; of additional heating, lighting, and other incidental costs arising from extended school activities; of capital adjustments, such as refurbishment, additional equipment, and enhanced security; and of transportation to enable children and other users to make use of the extended services.

Lessons distilled from experience with community schools

To date, a number of lessons have been learned through the community school experience. I have summarized these as follows:

Build consensus and partnership. Extending learning time at a school through programs such as tutoring in reading, homework centres, mentoring, or drug prevention will require collaboration among diverse partners. Not only parents and educators, but also community residents, service providers, and public officials will need — and want — to be involved. Programs should seek to draw on all of the community's resources while addressing the concerns of all partners.

Conduct a community assessment of needs and resources. A community assessment helps a partnership turn a shared vision for continuous learning and safety into strategies that use resources efficiently to address local conditions. Assessment information can come from interviews, surveys, focus groups, and community forums. All local stakeholders can contribute to the process so that the resulting strategies address real concerns and consider all possible resources.

Design programs with care. Successful partnerships have concluded that every school and community must choose its own combination of opportunities to address local conditions and concerns. Nevertheless, effective programs establish vision and focus, address needs in an appropriate manner, coordinate efforts, and from the beginning create a system of accountability.

Consider the details. School governance, liability, and building-maintenance issues are paramount in making a community school work. Strong leadership, collaborative decision making, and a clear understanding of management and organization procedures and policies such as liability, as well as managed, mutually acceptable arrangements for physical space, are elements of successful programs.

Provide effective staff. Staff for after-school or summer learning can come from the school, a partner agency, or the community, but should have appropriate experience, realistic expectations, and a true interest in caring for children. Paid professionals and teachers can be supplemented with volunteers and parents.

Evaluate a program's accomplishments. Community school programs are by nature complex and, no matter how well designed, must learn from experience. Continuous monitoring of a program's progress — in addition to a shared understanding of its goals — can help leaders and staff maintain their focus, improve effectiveness and accountability, ensure parent and participant satisfaction, and identify changes that need to be made. Continuous monitoring allows a program's director to assess whether key program features are working as intended.

So much for the main characteristics of community schools — or, to use my alternative designation, schools that show CARE (see appendix A). It is now time to offer some examples of these schools and programs, as well as a few examples of the teachers who work in them.

CHAPTER 4

Schools That Show CARE

I have always believed that schools can and do make a difference. In this chapter I look at representative schools that meet the basics of Caring, Accepting, Respecting, and Engaging (CARE) as set out in the first three chapters of this book. When appropriate, rather than describe these community hubs myself, I let those responsible for their success tell the story in their own words.

Much of my interest in schools that make a difference is in response to the 1966 study by James Coleman who concluded through his research that schools don't make a difference.

> Schools bring little influence to bear on a child's achievement that is independent of his background and general social context; this very lack of an independent effect means that the inequalities imposed on children by their home, neighborhood, and peer environment are carried along to become the inequalities with which they confront adult life at the end of school. For equality of educational opportunity must imply a strong effect of schools that is independent of the child's immediate environment, and that strong independent effect is not present in American schools.

The Coleman Report, *Inequality* by Christopher Jencks and colleagues (1972), and the Rand Corporation's *How Effective Is Schooling?* concluded that the family backgrounds of students — a variable designed to capture racial, economic, cultural, and community impacts on the cognitive development of children — exercised a far greater influence on children's scholastic achievement than their schooling experiences. The Rand study asked whether educational problems are really school problems, Averch and his colleagues (1972, vii) concluding, "The most profitable line of attack on educational problems may not, after all, be through the schools." These three studies have come to be known collectively as the Schools Don't Make a Difference research.

Now, one of the proper responses of the educational community to Coleman's discovery was to look inside the box of schooling, beneath macro-inputs, such as building and textbook quality, and to begin to examine school processes such as cultural bias and curricular tracking that have an impact on minority students in undesirable ways.

But I wish to look at a different response, more philosophical than empirical. While carrying out the Equality of Educational Opportunity study, Coleman proposed what philosophers would call a "consequentialist," results-oriented alternative to the traditional input-based conception of equal educational opportunity. His alternative involved measuring the presence or absence of equal educational opportunity by the equalization over time of average academic achievement between children of different racial and socioeconomic groups — in other words, lessening the achievement gap.

I believe that Coleman was on the right track, that perhaps children's total educational opportunities — those arising from family, community, and school — could be equalized by the powerful educative effects of formal schooling. Regardless of whether or not schools could deliver on this promise — the equal results standard — equal achievement across different racial and socioeconomic groups was clearly truer to the American attitude towards education than was equal inputs. Of course, no one expects that schools produce equal scholastic achievement for all individuals or for all individuals within any particular group. Given the obvious differences among persons in ability and aspirations, this standard would be impossible and even undesirable. Finally, no one expects perfect equality of achievement across groups in this generation or any other. As Charles Frankel put it, equality of educational opportunity implies "a direction of effort, not a goal to be achieved" (1971, 209).

What Produces Effective Education?

Parents want a good education for their children. Some may have greater resources or a more precise picture of how to accomplish their goal, but most parents in our society are aware that a good education is fundamental to financial, professional, and personal success. If we assume that this is true, why is it that so many of our students are doing so poorly? Many people feel that poverty, crime, and the breakdown of the family are an important part of the answer. Furthermore, research consistently reveals that parental income and educational success are the best indicators for predicting a child's educational achievement. Unfortunately, this is not something that schools have much of an impact on.

Recent research has discovered that after the socioeconomic well-being of the parents, the next most important variable predicting student success is the way in which a school is organized. Research has also established that effective schools have similar traits. Such schools have strong educational leaders who possess a clear vision of what it means to be an educated person and who have the authority to assemble a staff of like-minded teachers. These schools set high academic standards and encourage the belief that, with few exceptions, children are capable of achieving at high levels. They encourage collegial and professional staff relationships, and establish a disciplined and drug-free educational environment.

If we know what makes a school effective, how do we go about converting the vast number of ineffective schools? The expensive reforms of the last few decades have yielded marginal results. . . .

An example of an effective school is Westside Preparatory School in Chicago, where Marva Collins has proven that when the above criteria are met, students from low-income, single-parent families can achieve. In describing her inner-city program she states, "The expectations are as high here as in the most nurtured suburban area." Her motto for the students: "We are known by our deeds, not our needs."

An effective school is a school that can, in measured student achievement terms, demonstrate the joint presence of quality and equity. Said another way, an effective school is a school that can, in measured student achievement terms, demonstrate high overall levels of achievement and no gaps in the distribution of that achievement across major subsets of the student population. It has a learning-for-all mission. The seven correlates of effective schools are as follows: (1) a clear and focused mission, (2) a safe and orderly environment, (3) positive home–school relations, (4) frequent monitoring of student progress, (5) a climate of high expectations for success, (6) opportunity to learn and time on task, and (7) instructional leadership.

While the first-generation correlates of effective schools, stated above, provide an essential foundation if schools are to improve, the second generation, when successfully implemented, will move schools closer to the mission of learning for all. In *Getting By or Getting Better*, Wayne Hulley and Linda Dier outline the following first-to-second generation changes:

- a shift from teaching for all to learning by all;
- a shift to a stronger focus on cooperative learning, character education, social justice, and teamwork for both students and teachers;
- a shift from including parents and stakeholders to engaging them as meaningful partners to make a difference for every student;
- a shift to setting high expectations for teachers to ensure that intervention strategies, reteaching, regrouping, mentoring, and tutoring are included as measures to enable all students to attain improved outcomes;
- a shift to a stronger focus on formative assessment, recognized as a powerful strategy for informing teachers about instructional needs and involving students in their own learning;
- a shift to providing interventions in the classroom that will give struggling learners the extra time on task and additional opportunities to learn (narrowing the gap);
- a shift to the administrator becoming the "leader of leaders" and realizing that expertise resides in many people: teamwork, partnership, cooperation, and collaboration are the norm for instructional leadership.

The balance of this chapter presents a variety of schools that show CARE.

A Place of Second Chances: Winnipeg Adult Education Centre

Several accounts in this chapter, including this one, are based on interviews conducted by Jim Watt, a retired school superintendent, in 2007.

Opened in 1967, the Winnipeg Adult Education Centre (WAEC) provides adults with a second chance to graduate or improve their academic preparation for postsecondary pursuits. Principal Dushand Persuad makes this report:

WAEC has grown to the point that it offers a variety of programs for over 2200 adults each year. The student body is culturally and economically diverse, including large numbers of immigrants, Aboriginals, refugees, unemployed, and the working poor, all of whom try to improve their academic status and graduate with a high school diploma.

To enhance student success, many adaptations have been made to courses and scheduling and provision of academic supports and counselling, and multiple intake points. However, students identify the supportive staff and welcoming atmosphere as major reasons for their success. Staff has been known to consistently go "the extra mile" to afford students the opportunity to succeed.

The Basic Literacy Program at 700 Elgin Avenue offers upgrading to literacy skills from pre-readers up to grade 9. The students represent a diverse cultural mix of Aboriginal, Métis, refugees and immigrants from all over the globe. Aboriginal and Métis students are often residents of various northern remote communities. Most students are parents and/or grandparents. Generally, all of our students can be described as poor.

What is remarkable about the Basic Literacy Program is the high student attendance, the enthusiasm and success in elevating students' literacy skills. This is not surprising given extremely high staff enthusiasm and motivation that have resulted in the creation of a nurturing and welcoming school climate.

Each student is a story by him/herself. One that will stay forever with me is a male student explaining to a newcomer to the program about his reasons for making the daily one-hour trip to the program. He explained that he got tired of being put down for not being able to read his mail. He explained that one year later, he can now read his mail and more importantly he can now read small stories for his young grandchild.

The Adolescent Parent Centre (APC) is located in the old Cecil Rhodes Jr. High School at 136 Cecil Street. It is a unique educational program for 120 pregnant and parenting young girls/women up to the age of 21 who would otherwise not be in school and would most likely drop out. The ability to continue their education ensures a better life not only for themselves but also for their child.

Currently, a significant number of our students are Aboriginal and come from throughout Manitoba. The majority of our students are from the Winnipeg School Division, and the rest are from other school divisions and small communities outside Winnipeg. All of our students are presently at-risk, but many of them have been [so] throughout most of their school experience. Prior to becoming pregnant they were often poor attendees, were not academically successful, had been in trouble with the law, and had been involved with various agencies including Child and Family Services as a ward and now with their babies.

APC has created a wraparound support plan for our students and their babies. We want to empower them through the creation of powerful learning opportunities, hope for the future, and the involvement of extended families in the life of the school. We believe that involving partners and parents in the life of the school and in the learning process transfers into an enhanced ability to provide a caring, nurturing and language-enriched environment in the home. The positive relationships and the creation of a caring and nurturing school culture have contributed tremendously to having one of our largest graduating classes in the history of the school this year.

River Osborne Off Campus Site provides adults with the opportunity to graduate in a non-traditional setting. The off campus program is located in a local community centre and is geared towards adults who benefit from a small, supportive and nurturing school climate. Teacher–student ratio is small and the program offers an accommodating and flexible timetable. Student success is high, which is not surprising given the comfortable learning environment and the superb teachers.

Responsive Course Scheduling: Scott School, Regina

To describe the transformation of the oldest high school in Regina into a school that shows CARE, it is best to quote at length the staff:

To start the 2004 school year we had 204 students enrolled and we now [2006] have 400 students attending. We have doubled our population in a very short period of time which is amazing when you consider the crime rate, drug trafficking, abuse and poverty issues that can be identified in our area. Students are coming to school in spite of the problems they face every day.

We are running a quarter schedule here at the school. A number of years ago a change was made to move from the traditional semester system to a quarter system. The quarter system has a number of advantages. Students in our community tend to be very transient and move a great deal. What would happen is that the students were here for 2 months, they would move or drop out and lose their credits. A quarter system is approximately 2 and a half months long and allows each student to take 3 classes a day for about one hour and fifty minutes. If students did move after 2 months they have usually done enough to complete the credits and they would not lose the work or credits. In addition the quarter system allows youth more entry points, the opportunity to achieve 12 credits a year rather than the traditional 10 and therefore do some catch up over the course of the year, and because of the extended periods and time with the teacher, each student has more one on one time for assistance. It has been very successful with our students.

Teachers and staff at the school have worked very hard to create a sense of belonging with our students. As a result students are very accepting of each other and are here for the same reason — to learn. The school and community have been compared to a hurricane — we are the eye and the calm is noticeable as many of the societal issues swirl around us constantly. Very few students drop out. They may discontinue for a quarter but the school staff encourages and accepts the students, working with them on their time frame, not always the traditional one.

Another way in which Scott School has responded to its constituency is through its Re-entry program, organized by teacher Corey Matthews. It is not uncommon for students, especially of Aboriginal background, to drop out in Grade 9 and to re-enter school about two years later; this re-entry could be either court mandated or due to the youth recognizing the need to achieve a higher education. These youths however do not want to be in the regular Grade 9 program with students two or more years younger than they are. The Re-entry program engages them in school, letting them work at their own pace. Matthews individualizes instruction and works with students one on one to help them complete the curricular requirements for Grade 9 as quickly as possible. Students can then move into the Grade 10 program with others closer in age.

Mass Home Visits: St. John's High School, Winnipeg

At the beginning of the 2005–2006 school year, the vice-principal of St. John's High School in Winnipeg, Christine Penner, visited all 459 homes of Grades 7 and 8 students. Here is her account of what led up to these visits — and what flowed from them.

> St. John's is an inner-city high school with 1,200 students from grades 7–12.
>
> The students come from many different cultural, religious and ethnic backgrounds; many live in single-parent homes and approximately 60 per cent live below the poverty line. Drugs, gangs, violence and criminal activity are, sadly, a reality in the community.
>
> My philosophy has always been "If what you are doing is not working, change what you do!" In my first year as vice-principal of the Middle Years at St. John's I personally suspended 266 grade seven and eight students! Even though all suspensions were the result of violating our bottom lines, it did not take me long to figure out that what we were doing was not working. By suspending at-risk students we were often breaking the most solid connection these students had in their lives.
>
> In search of solutions, I put together a proposal for the 2005/2006 school year which included visiting all the homes of the Middle Years students. My thought was that if we wanted to affect change in behavior at school, we had to start in the home. The home visits provided me the opportunity to (1) meet all the parents on a positive note (too often we only contact parents on a negative note when their child has made a poor choice); (2) invite all parents to a parent meeting where I would explain the new restitution program we were going to implement that year, and to offer strategies on how we as educators and parents could work together to make the school and community a better place; and (3) welcome all grade seven students to St. John's, and answer any questions or address any fears they had about going to a big high school. In three weeks I visited 459 homes!
>
> The reaction by the parents and community was overwhelming. Parents warmly welcomed the home visits and clearly interpreted them as a message of care. Many parents were shocked to see me at their doorstep. Some of their comments included: "I am stunned!" "It's nice to see someone doing something about bullying" and "Anything with the word 'restitution' in it is good!" Parents seemed pleased to meet me and thrilled that the school was actively addressing some of their concerns. They were eager to be part of the solution to the many social problems in their neighborhood and in school. The home visits were a tangible way to make a strong connection between the school and the community.

"My thought was that if we wanted to affect change in behavior at school, we had to start in the home."

— Christine Penner

70

The home visits had a huge impact on parents, students, and the school in general. At our first parent meeting, where typically four or five parents showed up, we packed the theatre with 170 parents! At this time 20 parents signed up to volunteer, and we established monthly parent meetings. The media got wind of the home visits, resulting in good publicity for St. John's High School in the local papers, on TV, and on radio stations. Positive media coverage helped improve morale in school and in the community. The home visits helped develop a strong connection between parents and the school.

Although the home visits took me three weeks to complete, they were well worth the effort. By the end of the 2005/2006 school year the suspension rate of the Middle Years students at St. John's High School decreased by 20%! I believe that taking the time to visit all the homes of the grade seven and eight students was a contributing factor in bringing about this change. Making strong connections with parents/guardians, and showing students that we care were instrumental in creating a caring community within the school and helping students become better people and better citizens.

Opening Up Opportunities: York Street Public School, Ottawa

York Street Public School, which opened in 1921 in Ottawa, is now a model of a school that shows CARE. Jennifer Offord, as principal, made this report:

Today there are over 40 countries represented in our diverse population of approximately 265 students from Kindergarten to grade 8. Many of our families experience the stress and challenges associated with living in poverty. When an article last spring ranked schools according to their scores on the 2005 EQAO [Education, Quality, and Accountability Office] test, what it stated was that York was last. What it didn't state is what we're doing about it. The contributing factors are real (low socio-economic status, subsidized housing, single-parent families, transiency, first language at home is not English) but they are not excuses. Our students are able to achieve; we just need to do things differently. We need to make up for the skills they lack when they arrive at school and, according to brain research, we need to do it quickly.

We are currently participating in the Ministry Turnaround Project which focuses on raising literacy levels through the support of funding and the guidance of literacy experts. In less than a year, we have achieved the highest EQAO scores we've seen in the past five years — we're no longer last in the rankings. At York Street, we believe that our students not only deserve the same opportunities that other students have from more affluent neighbourhoods, but that they are entitled to them. Recreation and the arts are not considered "frills"; they are viewed as critical components to healthy child development and to a successful school experience. Our staff are constantly focusing on finding the potential in our students, the untapped talent that lies within each child.

With our community partners, we are constantly trying to level the playing field for our students, by removing financial barriers that exist

The school fund-raises to cover costs, including transportation and equipment.

"No, ma'am, I'm a readin' and writin' kind of kid."

See "Best Start Strategy, Ministry of Children and Youth Services, Ontario," in Chapter 5 for more detail on this program.

across our city (and province and country) and that exclude our students from participating in arts and recreation programs. Our philosophy is to provide effective programs for our students at no cost [to them]. For many of our students, experiences such as private music lessons, playing and traveling on a sports team, receiving tutoring, having a mentor, experiencing individual reading time with an adult, going to the National Arts Centre, attending summer camp, learning how to play chess, and attending an Ottawa 67's hockey game, are made possible because of York Street P.S. We see the benefits at school on a daily basis and improvements in the areas of attendance, behaviour and academic success.

In June 2006, three of our grade 8 students were accepted into the local high school for the arts, each in a different program.

The first student had previously been accepted into a gifted program at another school for grade 8, tried it briefly and then returned to York Street, feeling that he fit in better with his peers at our school. He is in the high school vocal program.

The second student arrived at York Street partway through the year from the southern United States. When I asked him what brought him to Ottawa, he said that his mother had died of an aneurysm and after living in several foster homes, he was almost adopted until they discovered that his biological father lived in Ottawa. [Since he was] dressed like an athlete, I also asked him if he was a sports kind of kid to which he responded, "No ma'am, I'm a readin' and writin' kind of kid." That was an understatement. His English teacher quickly discovered that he was a brilliant writer and she supported him through the application process. He is in the high school creative writing program.

The third student arrived at York Street from out of town with her father and younger brother. By grade 8 graduation, she was our master of ceremonies and received a collection of awards. She had benefited from participating on sports teams, our York Leadership Team, and was the lead in the annual musical. Her name is also signed beside two of our wall murals. She is in the high school visual arts program. Her Art teacher nominated her for an award, and at the ceremony in the fall, discovered that her family had moved during the summer to where the father could get a job and was living on the rural outskirts of Ottawa. By the time school started in September, the father had lost his job but clearly understood the importance of keeping the high school placement for his daughter. Until he found a place to live in the city, he and his daughter would hitchhike to the closest rural high school where she could catch a school bus to her high school. Now that's commitment and determination!

The day at York Street begins early and ends late. It's not unusual to see students arrive at school as early as 7:00 a.m. They may be attending the Best Start subsidized Daycare program for kindergarten-aged students that runs from 7:00 a.m. until 5:00 p.m., practicing piano or guitar, or meeting in the gym for sports, or eating in our Breakfast Program. We have an Adult ESL [English as a second language] class with on-site daycare in the morning. It's also not unusual to see students leave the school at 5:00 p.m. from our free daily afterschool program, the afterschool homework program supervised by volunteers from the

University of Ottawa's Somali Student Association, or from sports practice. Two of our teachers have won "Coach of the Year" for our region.

We are proud to provide private piano lessons to many of our students in grades 4, 5 and 6. What began as an offer for students from the University of Ottawa to teach our students piano has evolved into the "Heart of the City Piano Program," coordinated by our very dedicated and talented grade 5/6 teacher. Students are expected to commit to practice sessions in between their private piano lessons. This has become one of the most successful and beneficial programs in the school, with many of our students performing across the city. Their "gigs" include a recital at the University of Ottawa, a performance at the Chateau Laurier for the Kiwanis Club Annual General Meeting, and a performance at the launch event for the Education Foundation. Their teacher also takes his class to perform at our neighbouring seniors' residence. We are excited about the success of this program and the media attention that it has attracted, newspaper and radio. We were also thrilled with the donation of keyboards and pianos — when we ran out of room at the school for the pianos, we were able to put them directly into the students' homes.

Our annual volunteer and community luncheon appreciation event is held in the spring and the guest list is very long (up to 80) when you begin to consider all of the adults that contribute to the school through volunteering and through community partnerships and programs. These include the JUMP Math mentoring program, the OttawaREADS literacy program supported by employees from Bell Canada, and our mentoring programs. We host numerous student teachers from the University of Ottawa as well as students in high school or college who require co-op placements. Child & Youth Friendly Ottawa facilitated leadership training sessions for a group of our intermediate students. The Ottawa School of Speech and Drama has provided free acting lessons for our students.

We are always open to new ideas that fit into our philosophy. We are excited about three new opportunities this year. First, the City of Ottawa is introducing "Ultra Play," a free afterschool sports and activity program specifically targeted for students from low socio-economic backgrounds. Second, we are receiving a free inservice training session for all our intermediate students on how to play "Ultimate." Finally, our grade three students will be participating in a free program at our local swimming pool, called "Swim to Survive," which involves sessions focused on water safety.

Not only do we feel a responsibility for our students before and after school, we also look for opportunities for participation in summer activities. Our partnership with the Lowertown Community Centre allows students to play in a soccer league as well as an afternoon daycamp, both at no cost. I also recommend students to attend Christie Lake Camp, where they enjoy two weeks of camping and skill development. It began in 1922 specifically for underprivileged kids, and it continues today with the same mission. We are fortunate to have a place for our most needy students to spend two weeks in the summer, often their best two weeks.

Helping our students have a successful school experience isn't just a nice thing to do — it's the right thing to do. What we need is "informed passion" — having both the emotional drive and motivation to do what is right, balanced with the knowledge and research to know what is right.

We build self-esteem through skill-development and continue to remove financial barriers that exclude our most vulnerable children from opportunities that other children have, particularly in the areas of arts and recreation. It's a challenge, a privilege, and extremely rewarding. The relationships we develop with our students are based on caring and trust — and lots of humour . . . school is a place to celebrate childhood.

Turning Around Together: Sir Winston Churchill Secondary School, Hamilton

Like York Street Public School in Ottawa, Sir Winston Churchill Secondary School in Hamilton has made the transition into a school that shows CARE, particularly for at-risk students who all too often fall through the cracks of our education system. The person who led the way in Churchill's remarkable turnaround is its principal, Peter Joshua. This is his account of how the transformation was accomplished:

I find myself in my office at Sir Winston Churchill Secondary School reflecting upon the incredible journey I have shared with a dynamic staff, dedicated parents, and a wonderful group of students, as we enjoy together the success that has come with necessary change over the past four years. As a leader, I have had the unique opportunity to recognize and celebrate the strengths of so many enthusiastic individuals as we continue to bring a shared vision forward into action. Because of their outstanding commitment, I can confidently say that Churchill Secondary is the best school in the Hamilton-Wentworth District School Board, and I am fortunate to share in its overwhelming richness.

My journey began when I arrived on the doorstep of this modest building in July of 2003. A composite high school in the east end of Hamilton, Churchill was viewed as a typical inner-city institution: low achievement and literacy scores, a high student mobility rate of over 48%, 54% of families with a single parent, and deemed as a high needs school in terms of socio-economic status. Across the grade levels, an average of 76.8% of the students were considered "at-risk" based on failure rates in Math, Science or English, and an absenteeism rate of greater than 15%. I saw a community with several modest dwellings and small businesses surrounding the school, and gang activity was a part of life, particularly in the subsidized housing complexes only a few yards away. It was no surprise that our students struggled with general apathy and a lack of commitment to the learning environment they were offered.

Despite these apparent roadblocks, I noticed that our staff worked tirelessly to provide students with the best experience they could possibly receive. In those early days of my Churchill experience, the road seemed uphill for so many. Our parents were often distant and felt unwelcome. Our School Council consisted of 3 members — one parent, a community representative and the principal. Staff, although motivated and talented, seemed often to work in isolation. Individual departments did not seem to collaborate with each other on several policies such as behavioural management and instructional practice. Many students commented on Churchill's lack of success in sports and their general disinterest in school

"I remember a feeling of elation and excitement that somehow I was exactly where I needed to be. In this building there was positive energy and a sense of hope that could not be ignored."

— Peter Joshua

activities and social events. The school struggled to hold onto a population of under 900 students and, as such, was often understaffed in the office and in terms of external support. The administrative team of two was seen to be inadequate for the number of emerging behavioural issues that challenged the staff on a daily basis. Police commented on the unusually high number of fights and drug issues; constant suspensions and office referrals made it quite apparent that we were putting out fires as quickly as they burst into flames before us.

I remember a feeling of elation and excitement that somehow I was exactly where I needed to be. In this building, there was positive energy and a sense of hope that could not be ignored. After a summer of reviewing statistics, school protocols and practices, I eagerly began the school year as a brand new principal. I felt supported and welcomed by all and it was time to roll up my sleeves and get down to business.

As early as those first days, I recall how willing the staff was to join me in a search for a shared mission and vision. We started by reviewing our beliefs and values and I challenged them to question what we were trying to accomplish at Churchill. I knew that if we were going to change and rise above our perceived status in the educational world, we would need to become a learning community determined to collaborate together for the sake of our students.

Our shared mission and vision began with this statement: "Sir Winston Churchill Secondary School is committed to providing students with a safe, structured, nurturing environment that allows them to gain knowledge and life-long skills, so that they may develop to their full potential and positively contribute to society."

A nurturing environment for all meant that anyone walking into this building would feel a sense of warmth and see a place for positive learning. Our incredible caretaking staff took this statement to heart and was the first to demonstrate a sense of pride for their school. Our floors gleamed and our walls were freed of graffiti and brightened with a fresh coat of paint. Thanks to teachers, our hallways were decorated with student work; display cases were beginning to fill up with student awards and achievements; clocks were upgraded to include a student-designed school logo; and we increased our supply of computers so that more labs were available for both student and teacher use. Our dedicated office staff strived to develop a flawless communication system so that parents and students would be informed and ready to collaborate with teachers on this new journey towards increased student success. We were certainly well on our way to establishing the changes necessary to ensure learning for all students.

In my role as principal, I recognized how extremely fortunate I was to be working with a vibrant group of teaching, office and caretaking staff. We continued our journey together in accordance with our school board's initiative to support and build an effective school based on the research of Lawrence W. Lezotte. We studied his concepts carefully and, as a united team of both teaching and non-teaching staff, we developed an action plan to align ourselves according to his prescribed correlates of effective schools. Departments were speaking the same language and we focused our professional development on the value of these correlates, including instructional leadership, a safe and orderly environment, a climate of high expectations for success, and a positive relationship with our parents.

As a professional learning community, teachers set out to increase their efforts as instructional leaders. With the unique experience of chairing our board's Assessment and Evaluation Committee, I was able to support them in the development of a solid and consistently delivered curriculum. We have seen a move to increase the use of assessment strategies so that students are provided with constant feedback as they take ownership of assignments and tasks, and teachers are focused on the concept of assessment for learning. At this time, I can proudly say that 100% of our staff has incorporated this concept into their teaching, an increase from less than 50% four years ago. Using the method of data-based decision making, each teacher developed goals to increase student achievement on tests and assignments, and we have seen a rise of 7 to 10% across several classrooms. I am even more amazed by our success in literacy development.

We were once struggling with EQAO test scores of 48% in February of 2003. Staff was resigned to the fact that because of the socio-economic status and the literacy rate in the community, we would continue to perform as one of the lowest scoring schools in the board and province. Our literacy team was largely comprised of members of the English department and other teachers did not see the relevance of the test or development of literacy within their curriculum. I immediately supported the concept that the team needed new energy and a solid literacy action plan. Members from every department were encouraged to join the Literacy Committee. Reading and writing strategies across all curricula were quickly developed and implemented by all departments and we pursued several opportunities to connect with grade 7 and 8 teachers in our feeder schools to talk about the literacy continuum. An after-school literacy remediation program was set up for students who needed the extra support; retired teacher volunteers were invited to act as one-on-one mentors for students at the greatest risk of failure; and we received funding to set up a literacy computer lab so that technology would allow us to primarily engage our male population. The results were astounding! In the following year, we saw an increase of 12% success for first time eligible students writing the OSSLT [Ontario Secondary School Literacy Test] and we were recognized as one of the most improved schools in Ontario.

By the year 2005, we had increased our scores to 75% success for all students. We had the highest rate of achievement for boys in the board and we were profiled on the provincial EQAO website as a Secondary School success story. Most importantly, our staff and students now appreciate the importance of literacy as part of all curricula, taught in all classrooms.

Our parent group became vital in ensuring that we would indeed become an effective school. With the indescribable support and drive of an amazing school council chair, I had the unique pleasure of building a parent group from its humble beginning of three members to its current enrolment of 15. These parents embraced the concept of building positive relationships and have been extremely instrumental in bridging a gap that in the past has kept our parents from participating so necessarily in their students' success. We began by surveying our larger parent popula-

"Our parent group became vital in ensuring that we would indeed become an effective school. With the indescribable support and drive of an amazing school council chair, I had the unique pleasure of building a parent group from its humble beginning of three members to its current enrolment of 15."

— Peter Joshua

tion so that we could clearly identify their needs and issues surrounding our apparently intimidating institution. After successfully pursuing a grant and partnership with the Hamilton Community Foundation, we developed a communication series entitled "Let's Connect — Plugging in to Churchill." Parents were invited to attend workshops based on their concerns, but, more importantly, we set out to break down barriers and provide a safe, nurturing environment for these caregivers so that their students would have a greater chance for success. This was an invaluable experience where we allowed parents to make a connection with the school and with our community partners such as Alternatives for Youth, Public Health, and our local police. We tackled issues such as drug and alcohol abuse, healthy active living and support for families struggling with student absenteeism and homework apathy. Our school council of parents organized childcare, nourishment and gift incentives, whatever it took to draw our community towards us. The series was overwhelmingly successful and I knew that we had begun to break down these imposing barriers.

As a continuation, I provided an opportunity for our school council parents to work closely with staff as part of our learning community. These committed parents attended several meetings with staff as we looked for ways to build positive relationships between home and school. Ideas were immediately put into action as we organized a family information night and free barbecue in our school cafeteria. Over a thousand people attended this highly successful event; the room was filled with excitement and conversation. This was a wonderful opportunity for parents to meet our staff on a social level and talk about ways that they could volunteer and support our school programs. As a result, we had teachers boasting about new connections and partnerships with parents, and the next parent interview night had a record 30% increase in attendance.

The parents on our school council were also instrumental in our lobby for additional administrative support. Through letter writing and campaigning with our board superintendent and trustee, we were able to successfully hire another vice principal, a move I felt was critical in our efforts to support staff and students in developing an effective and proactive discipline code. Students were encouraged and supported for positive behaviour. Office referrals were dealt with quickly and we made a commitment to reduce the absenteeism and lateness among our students. Through the implementation of an in-school suspension room, our administrative team saw an immediate reduction in lateness to class by 27%. Our suspension rate also dropped by 19% and we knew that our contacts with parents and community agencies were on a steady rise. Regular collaboration with community policing resulted in a decrease in drug busts and violent incidents reported to us yearly by our police liaison officer. These were all recognized by our staff as the necessary steps to ensure a safe and orderly environment. Everywhere in the school, we talked the language of consistent practice so that all of our learners knew what to expect and knew that they had to take responsibility for their education . . . .

By this point, I had my feet firmly planted as principal, knowing that Churchill Secondary School was on its way to becoming a phenomenal centre for learning. This was now a time when our province was clearly promoting their student success initiatives, namely the 4 pillars of literacy, numeracy, pathways, and character education. I was confident that in our effort to become instructional leaders in a climate of high expectations, staff, students and parents knew the value of literacy and numeracy skills, and the importance of building strong pathways toward life-long learning and success.

Character education to us meant the presence of a caring adult for every student who walked through our doors. Our commitment to a positive learning environment meant that we had to tackle that which stood in the way for many of our clientele — for some it was poverty, for others the lack of mental and social well-being. Staff and parents were once again united to break down these seemingly insurmountable walls.

Through the support of funding from various partners such as Dofasco Steel, the Hamilton Optimist Club, Tim Hortons, East Hamilton Rotary Club, and Hamilton Partners in Nutrition, Churchill established its "Nourishing Minds" nutrition program. Here, student volunteers serve breakfast and lunch to any students who choose to access the program, regardless of need. Teachers and parents now regularly serve hot after-school meals in a welcoming atmosphere where students can come to complete homework or simply relax.

Once again, due to the commitment of volunteers and partners such as the Hamilton East Lions Club, we also opened a "Walk-in Clothing Closet" program, providing gently used clothing and toiletries to our needy students and families. Several staff and students embraced this concept of support for our needy by developing a "Care Committee." Their initiatives include a Christmas dinner and food basket for our own struggling students, but most importantly, they instill the message that we all need to take care of each other. I am always humbled by the experience of watching these people reach out to help one another.

As part of our student success action plan, I have worked with staff to initiate a teacher–student mentoring program for our most at-risk students; we have also established an alternative education program complete with independent study packages, learning strategy modules, and an opportunity for co-op and experiential learning. Furthermore, we have a unique connection with the Learning Partnership through the provision of a "Change Your Future" counsellor who provides one-on-one support for a number of students struggling to find their direction. This has all inevitably resulted in an increased level of success for students. For example, our failure rates for Math and Science at the applied level have decreased by 10–15% over the past year and more students in grades 9 and 10 are remaining in school to complete their credits.

Finally, I must reflect on the importance of our student leadership. We pride ourselves on establishing this successful environment where students are encouraged to act as leaders in their community. Student Council has grown to include members representing all clubs and athletics. By carefully surveying the needs of their peers, this dynamic force has set out to increase the level of spirit and involvement in every school event. Our first dance of the year had a record attendance, increased by 75% from previous years; school teams have been bringing home more city championship trophies than we have seen in many years; our

"Several staff and students embraced this concept of support for our needy by developing a 'Care Committee.' Their initiatives include a Christmas dinner and food basket for our own struggling students, but most importantly, they instill the message that we all need to take care of each other."

— Peter Joshua

See Chapter 5 for detail on the Change Your Future program, as well as on the Walk-in Closet, mentioned above.

Recreation Leadership class has organized successful events for elementary schools and special needs students across our board; several students have represented our fine school in overseas trips to various parts of Europe; we have established an award-winning student environmental program that has received provincial recognition; and we finish every school year with a celebration assembly so that everyone feels the power and energy that comes with success. A few weeks back, as I stood on our home field during one of our football games, a fellow staff member leaned over to me and commented on the fact that we had not had such an event for seven years. As I looked around at the excitement of many cheering faces painted in school colours, players striving to gain that extra yard, and parents glowing with admiration, I was filled with pride as I realized how this once quiet, hidden treasure of a school had emerged and found its rightful place on the map!

As we look to our future, there is no greater evidence of success than our enrolment increase from 887 to our current figure of 1125 students. These are people who want to come to school to learn and to be accepted. Our learning teams are looking forward and they are finding the need to dig a little deeper into achievement data. We now challenge ourselves to analyze where our students come from and what their destinations seem to be. We continually strive to achieve that environment where all students are fully engaged and on the right path to their individual goals and aspirations.

In my particular path to this wonderful school, I happened upon a very appropriate quotation from Sir Winston Churchill in a parliamentary speech he once gave, and I'd like to close by sharing it with you: "Every day you may make progress. Every step may be fruitful. Yet there will stretch out before you an ever-lengthening, ever-ascending, ever-improving path. You know you will never get to the end of the journey. But this, so far from discouraging, only adds to the joy and glory of the climb." At this school named in his honour, I cherish the very fact that together, we strive to help all students towards their path of success and hope that their climb will be a joyful and glorious one.

A Well-Entwined Partnership: Queen Mary Elementary School, Hamilton

The Hamilton East Kiwanis Boys and Girls Club and Queen Mary Elementary School enjoy a great partnership. During Queen Mary renovations in 1996, the school used the Kiwanis facility; when the Kiwanis club was rebuilt, it used the school to run its programs. Hamilton East Kiwanis also supports the school's nutrition program, one of the largest in the province.

The Queen Mary–Kiwanis partnership serves approximately 80 percent of the students through homework clubs, computer classes, and after-school programs that are run largely by retired teachers. The partnership provides a wonderful example of institutions helping students develop the skills and competencies they need to succeed as adults.

As is true of the Queen Mary community, we cannot afford to let children and their families receive discrete, unconnected services from a number of agencies or organizations working in isolation from each other. We need to work together.

Integrated School-Linked Services: Nutana Collegiate, Saskatoon

Nutana Collegiate, which opened its doors in 1909, is the oldest collegiate in the city of Saskatoon, Saskatchewan. Its staff report that "the collegiate functioned in a traditional format until the 1990s when it became apparent that such a model no longer supported the needs of students or the community. The school transformed in many ways and now operates with an Integrated School-Linked Services model and a quartered as opposed to a semestered school year." Their account continues:

"Employees from a variety of agencies such as health, mental health, addictions, social services, advanced education, justice, restorative justice, youth engagement and child care are in the school either full-time or on a regular basis to serve the needs of students where students spend their day."

As of September 30, 2006, there were approximately 650 students attending the collegiate in Grades 9 to 12, with the majority of students aged 18 and over and coming to the school from every area of the city. Some students attend to upgrade marks in particular classes while others are completing graduation credits or doing an adult program. These students are supported not only by teachers in their academic work, but also by a host of service providers from government and non-profit agencies and many community business partners.

The Integrated School-Linked Services [ISLS] model brings a true community approach to education into the school. Employees from a variety of agencies such as health, mental health, addictions, social services, advanced education, justice, restorative justice, youth engagement and child care are in the school either full-time or on a regular basis to serve the needs of students where students spend their day. These agencies work closely together for the benefit of youth and families and use available funding more effectively to address needs which are beyond the professional mandate of educators. The ISLS model offers an approach to planning and service delivery that is more coordinated, comprehensive and responsive to the complex and diverse needs of students and families. The model also requires shared leadership for planning, decision making, resources and evaluation . . .

What They Are Not About	*What They Are About*
single agency focus	collaboration and partnerships
limited community involvement	broad-based community
focus on maintenance of	involvement
structures over client needs	focus on addressing needs of
top-down mandated change and	children at-risk
control	responsiveness
single organization leadership or	shared leadership and ownership
responsibility	community-based (bottom-up)
hiring of coordinating staff	change initiative and
single mandated model with	management
little real change	better use made of resources in
"tinkering at the edges"	the community
	coordination and collaboration
	built into everyone's job
	revised mandates, roles, and job
	descriptions
	empowerment of field-level staff
	new ways of delivering services
	fluid and flexible structures,
	processes, and procedures
	fundamental change

Nutana Collegiate works with a wide range of ISLS partner agencies to meet the many needs of families served. Among the agencies are Saskatoon Health Region (a full-time nurse practitioner); Department of Community Resources (provincial — a full-time social worker); Department of Advanced Education (provincial — a full-time adult career consultant); Youth Launch (federal — two adult facilitators and contracted youth workers); Child Care Centre for 17 children operated by a non-profit board with seven employees; Parent Centre (operated with 1.5 full-time staff to offer programming and support for teen parents); John Howard Society (one half-day per week with two employees offering counselling, addiction services, and restorative work); Department of Corrections (provincial — a corrections worker one half-day per week); Family Services (provincial — a half-time community worker); Mental Health (provincial — one half-day per week of counselling services); and the University of Saskatchewan (a full-time researcher for the 2006–2007 school year).

Other programs and supports offered by Nutana include three satellite programs within Saskatoon. Omega, in downtown Saskatoon, offers programming for youth 16 and older who have anger-management issues. Mainstreet, located a few blocks away from Nutana in a business district, focuses on youth under 16 with behavioral problems. SAGE, located in downtown Saskatoon, serves youth aged 12 to 16 coming out of custody. Its outreach activities include holding a classroom in an adolescent mental-health resource centre; having a teacher work with youth admitted to Royal University Hospital; and supply a teacher to work at an addictions treatment centre operated by the province.

The teaching staff has also created innovative new programming for students, such as tourism (associated with the Canadian Academy of Travel and Tourism), wildlife management, and visual arts with a focus on Aboriginal art. A fourth program, career and work exploration, is extensive.

Several business partners work with Nutana Collegiate. They "offer a variety of services such as adult mentoring, volunteer and employment positions, class presentations, funding of various programs and initiatives." Over time, partners have included SaskTel, the Saskatoon Credit Union, the Saskatoon Prairieland Exhibition, the *Star Phoenix*, the Saskatchewan Tourism Education Council, St. Paul's Hospital, and Wanuskewin Heritage Park.

In summary, Nutana Collegiate "is committed to flexible, creative programming that helps youth to be successful in school both at our campus and in a variety of other community settings. The teachers value the support and teamwork with colleagues from a variety of other agencies and institutions. Together we can do our best work with youth."

"Relative to the latter [professional learning], we concluded that breakthrough results were not possible unless each and every teacher was learning how to improve every day."

— Michael Fullan, *The Six Secrets of Change*

See Appendix A, "Criteria for Schools That Show CARE," for a checklist that allows you to assess whether your school fits the description of a school that shows CARE or whether it is a candidate for transformation.

As you have read, there are people succeeding against the odds and producing magnificent results in extremely difficult circumstances.

The problem we have in education is that we have never found an effective way to replicate such success. That is partly because the magic of education is always what happens in the individual classroom between the teacher and the student, supported by the parents and strengthened by a school culture set overwhelmingly by a gifted principal.

I know that.

But there have to be ways to recognize the plain fact that, notwithstanding the funding problems, notwithstanding the inequalities, notwithstanding all the problems in public education, if you look at enough schools, you can find virtually every problem in our country solved by somebody somewhere in an astonishingly effective fashion.

So, the challenge for us here is to figure out how to replicate that.

CHAPTER 5

Programs That Show CARE

This chapter, like Chapter 4, offers examples of educational instruction that show CARE. The focus this time, however, is more on programs than on schools. The distinction, of course, is not meant to suggest a basic difference — only a school that shows CARE can operate a program that shows CARE; the characteristics and objectives of the two are identical. Both place the needs of students first, both embrace an approach to teaching and learning that follows the principle of Caring, Accepting, Respecting, and Engaging, and both aim at the creation of a school climate that places education in the broader context of community life.

As in Chapter 4, whenever appropriate, I let those responsible for the programs that show CARE describe those programs in their own words.

Woodward Summer Reading Program, Hamilton

Need: To maintain student reading levels over the summer

Community Connection: Redhill Public Library

Every September, the staff at Woodward Junior Public School in Hamilton noticed that the reading skill levels of the majority of their students — students who could ill afford to lose the reading gains of the previous year — declined over the summer. As a result of the "summer reading slump," valuable learning time was lost during the first several weeks of school as teachers helped their students make up lost ground.

Staff believed that reading scores would remain stable or even increase if they could keep their students reading at least three times a week throughout July and August so they launched a reading program. The Woodward Summer Reading Program began as a joint effort between teaching staff, support staff, volunteers, and funding partners. It is linked with the public library, to which easy access is not possible for many students. Through this link students gain not only a venue for borrowing books, but an opportunity to borrow books at their level through a tracking system.

The program does more than enable students to read. It provides a setting in which they can also learn how to engage in comprehension and word attack strategies. Further, their parents can observe trained personnel working with their children. With each year that it has operated, the Summer Reading Program has grown, providing service to more than 60 students daily in 2007.

As the following account, provided by Principal Joyce Munro, indicates, the results have been striking:

DRA (Developmental Reading Assessment) is a reading assessment tool that applies to students from Kindergarten to Grade 8. It enables teachers to identify individual student needs and it informs instruction. DRA enables teachers to analyze reading comprehension and determine proficiency, set instructional goals for each student, and document student progress.

Participating staff members (90 percent) came away with a strong feeling of success and fulfillment, knowing that their generous contribution of time and expertise during their summer vacation did indeed make a difference to their students.

Needs: Hunger, clothing

Community Connections: Rotary Club, Hamilton Foundation

None of the students who attended the program on a consistent basis (75 percent of the time) lost ground and the majority (66 percent) increased their DRA [Developmental Reading Assessment] reading level. Early readers (junior and senior kindergarten) demonstrated a notable improvement in reading readiness skills such as book handling skills and picture reads. Parents and caregivers were given a unique opportunity to see effective reading support in action as they observed trained personnel work with their children. We have heard from parents that this improved their abilities to read purposefully with their children at home (unlocking unfamiliar words, prompting retells, using effective questioning skills to develop comprehension).

Participating staff members (90 percent) came away with a strong feeling of success and fulfillment, knowing that their generous contribution of time and expertise during their summer vacation did indeed make a difference to their students. The students themselves felt a great deal of pride in their accomplishments. Community connections were established with the Redhill Public Library, which supported the program with additional recognition and rewards. Students from other schools and even one from another school board attended. The Hamilton *Spectator* ran an excellent piece on the program, which was not only a positive thing for our school but for summer literacy in general.

Breakfast and the Walk-in Closet, Hamilton

Sir John A. Macdonald Secondary School in Hamilton offers a breakfast program for underprivileged students. Students file past a long buffet of cereal, toast, buns, yogurt, and juice. They each fill their plates and bowls, then walk to tables and eat their meals. Without breakfast at school, these children might otherwise go hungry.

The long-term intention of breakfast programs, like this one, is to break the cycle of poverty by levelling the playing field for many children from low-income families. Providing breakfast at school promotes improved classroom behavior, reduces absenteeism, and helps enable students to better retain and learn new information. The program at Sir John A. Macdonald is funded through the generosity of the Rotary Club, with a portion of the funding coming from the Breakfast for Learning program administered by the Hamilton Foundation.

A partner program, to which the Rotary Club also provides funding, is called the Walk-in Closet. Two rooms at the secondary school are stocked with winter coats, boots, non-perishable food, and toiletries. The school is continually buying new socks, underwear, and toothpaste. On a regular basis, teachers of the school go shopping for the Walk-in Closet, spending their own money.

A Pathway to Success

Pathways to Education was created as a responsive intervention that has both short-term and long-term effects. It began in Toronto's Regent Park with the mission of breaking the cycle of poverty and unemploy-

Need: To keep disadvantaged, at-risk students in school and promote postsecondary education

Community Connections: Among the long list of partners are universities, including York, Toronto, and Ryerson; George Brown College; school boards, including Toronto District and Toronto Catholic; churches, such as St. Paul's Catholic; missions, such as Yonge Street and Frontier College; businesses, such as Royal Bank, TD Bank Financial Group, and Stikeman Elliott LLP, Toronto; more than 60 individual public and high schools; and not-for-profit groups, Soulpepper Theatre Company and Black Students Association among them.

ment there. It provides a unique blend of educational, social and financial supports that economically disadvantaged, at-risk kids in the community need to get to school, stay in school, succeed in school and move on to postsecondary programs. The Pathways to Education Program also has a vision of community succession. In Regent Park, for example, the Regent Park Community Health Centre (RPCHC) hopes that twenty years from now, the kids in the Pathways to Education Program will be the doctors, nurses, social workers, and executive directors of the health centre and in this community, transforming it from within and restoring it to overall health.

The Pathways program consists of four core components:

1. Staff enter into a contract with the students, their parents, and the school boards that establish clear expectations and accountabilities.
2. They engage volunteers in providing after-school tutoring and mentoring.
3. Their support workers help students seize opportunities and cope with issues they may be facing.
4. They provide the financial support needed to reduce barriers to success in high school and make it easier for a transition into postsecondary school.

The Pathways to Education Program has gone from serving 76 students from 16 high schools in its first year to serving 828 students from 55 high schools at time of writing. In its more than eight years of operation, it has had these successes:

- Before the program got under way, the dropout rate in Regent Park was 56 percent—it is now below 10 percent.
- Of 462 youth who have gone through the Pathways Program and completed high school, 367 of those graduates (80 percent) have gone into postsecondary education.
- More than 80 percent of high school graduates going to postsecondary school are the first in their family to do so.
- The attrition rate for Pathways students in university is 1.8 percent, well below the 16 percent average.
- The attrition rate for Pathways students in college is 9.3 percent, well below the 25 percent average.
- Participation in postsecondary education has quadrupled from the pre-Pathways rate of 20 percent up to 80 percent.

Mentoring Matters

Student Mentoring Educational Assistant Program

The Student Mentoring Educational Assistant Program, which began in 2005, is founded on the belief that all students deserve every opportunity to reach their full potential. The program, which works in group settings or one to one, assists students in achieving academic, social, and emotional success in a supportive, safe, and encouraging environment.

It helps students in overcoming personal/social barriers and empowers them to develop the skills to become lifelong learners and respectful citizens. Student Mentoring EAs are currently working with 160 Grades 6 and 7 students deemed "at-risk" at inner-city schools. So far, the Student Mentoring Educational Assistant Program has made a positive difference in the lives of more than 450 students, who owe much to the dedication and commitment of program members.

Project G.O. (Girls Only)

This program, similar to the Boys to Men initiative, has been successful in making a difference in the lives of young women. Project G.O. was designed to provide mentorship and positive role models for at-risk female students in Grades 6 to 8.

Many of these young girls are in need of a strong female model in their lives to assist in the challenges during their teenage years. Project G.O. pairs teachers and educational assistants with girls so that they can talk through issues of self-esteem and anti-bullying to name a few.

The teachers and educational assistants serving as mentors are dedicated to making a positive difference within the lives of more than 160 at-risk youth who attend inner-city schools. Janet Alder says, "The purpose of the program is to assist students in achieving their full potential socially, emotionally and academically, in a supportive, safe and encouraging environment." The mentors help the girls to apply themselves in planning and decision making that incorporates their personal interests, strengths, abilities, and accomplishments.

At one Project G.O. session at Delta Secondary School in Hamilton, Ontario, hundreds of middle-school girls were encouraged to start a chain reaction of kindness by taking Rachel's Challenge. Rachel Scott was the first victim of the Columbine massacre in the United States, and her legacy has laid the foundation for the most life-changing school program in North America. Students are challenged to make a difference in their schools by embracing five key elements: (1) eliminating prejudice, (2) daring to dream, (3) choosing your influences,(4) using kind words, and (5) starting a chain reaction with families and friends. As Rachel once wrote, "I have this theory that if one person can go out of their way to show compassion, then it will start a chain reaction of the same."

The girls listened to a powerful presentation about Rachel's life and learned about ways they could implement Rachel's Challenge in their own schools and girls clubs. After the presentation, more than 200 girls signed a banner pledging their commitment to take Rachel's Challenge back to their own schools.

Change Your Future

Need: Academic success

Community Connections: Learning Partnership, Royal Bank of Canada

Change Your Future (CYF), an innovative Canada-wide educational program offered by the Learning Partnership, is designed to increase students' chances of success in school. The program provides essential support and encouragement to racially diverse students and students from Aboriginal communities, with the goal of helping them stay in school and plan their futures. Program counsellors are placed in schools 1.5 days per week and work with school staff to help participating students in Grades 7 to 10 overcome barriers, make the right decisions, set goals, build confidence, and engage in a self-help and discovery process. In 2005 the Royal Bank of Canada, a supporter of the Learning Partnership since its inception, donated $300 000 over three years to the CYF.

Eligibility requirements for the CYF program are broad. The program accepts students who come from minority ethnic groups and Aboriginal communities; who have shown potential for academic success; who have expressed a desire to do well in school and develop their aspirations; who have a record of poor attendance or late arrival at school; who have demonstrated poor organizational and study skills; who have the ability to function within the context of a peer group; who respond well to encouragement and support; who would benefit from a positive adult role model; and who need help in accessing resources and support to achieve greater success in school.

The Summer Literacy Program

It is a well-known fact that students who live in poverty lose two to three reading levels over the summer. Summer Literacy was founded the summer of 2001 by teacher Rob Blunsdon in partnership with the Hamilton-Wentworth District School Board, the Rotary Club of Hamilton, and YWCA Hamilton to bridge the learning gap that affects students who live in poverty over the summer. It follows the comprehensive literacy model but is focused on fun. The program has evolved every summer in response to an extensive evaluation model.

Summer Literacy began with two goals: to maintain or improve each participant's developmental reading level as evaluated at the beginning of the program and to improve attitudes towards school and learning as first evaluated. If these expected outcomes are met, it means that participants will have more positive self-images and become productive members of the school community. Assessment is based on five components: participant background and feedback; attitude towards reading; attendance; parent feedback; and running records for a sample group of 25 percent of students, three per student.

The Summer Literacy Program has proven to be highly successful. Program attendance and capacity have risen from 51 participants in 2001 to 1077 in 2008. The program has expanded from a three-week half-day program to a six-week full-day program offering participants the options of three different two-week sessions.

The key to the program's success is using the data from completed assessments to improve the program. With the running record focus groups, the success rate of students who maintain or improve their June DRA level is 89.24 percent.

Robert Blunsdon, the director of the program since 2002, writes:

Every year I strive to help students who live in poverty feel and become more successful at school. The program is completely free and every year I

The Learning Partnership is the only not-for-profit organization in Canada dedicated to bringing together business, education, government, labour, policy makers, and the community to develop partnerships that strengthen public education in Canada.

Need: To maintain or improve students' reading levels over the summer

Community Connections: Rotary Club of Hamilton, YWCA Hamilton, and Focus on Youth (a provincial ministry initiative that provides funding)

work hard to improve the program on very little budget. "Service above self" is the philosophy of the program. I believe this passion is what increases enrollment every year and the families we work with respect that we listen to them and value their input.

Adopt a Village

Need: Global education

Community Connection: Free the Children

Like many other boards in the province of Ontario, the Hamilton-Wentworth District School Board (HWDSB) has embarked on an exciting board-wide partnership with Free the Children through the Adopt a Village campaign. Free the Children is the largest network of children helping children through education in the world, with more than one million youth involved in their innovative education and development programs in 45 countries. Founded by Canadian child-rights activist Craig Kielburger and his brother, Marc, Free the Children has an established track record of success, with three nominations for the Nobel Peace Prize and partnerships with the United Nations and Oprah Winfrey's Angel Network. Since 1989, Free the Children has worked in partnership with school boards on numerous successful education activities.

The partnership between the HWDSB and Free the Children is intended to accomplish three main objectives: (1) to allow Hamilton-Wentworth students from both the elementary and secondary levels to make a lasting difference in the lives of children around the world; (2) to enable the students to participate in unprecedented cross-cultural communication, exchange opportunities, and curriculum-enhancing opportunities; and (3) to provide Hamilton-Wentworth students, educators, administrators, and support staff with an opportunity to become globally involved in tangible ways.

Taking part in this program allows students to see that poverty is relative — partner schools likely lack clean water! — and to come to understand that an injustice anywhere is a threat to justice everywhere.

The Adopt a Village campaign supports integrated and holistic community-development projects to help marginalized children and their families meet basic human needs: access to education, health care, clean water, quality sanitation, and economic opportunities. Target countries for the program are Kenya, Sierra Leone, China, and Sri Lanka. Through the campaign, schools will be able to

- build a "partner" school in a developing country through a fundraising program;
- support the partner school and its community through the provision of health care, teacher wages, and health programs;
- visit the partner school;
- benefit from a motivational-speaking program at schools — at no cost — on issues related to student leadership opportunities, community development, and the campaign itself;
- interact and connect with the students in the partner school when applicable; and
- learn throughout the process with curriculum materials provided by Free the Children.

Alternative Education Program/Expulsion Program, Hamilton

Need: Re-engage students in school

Community Connections: Local corporate sponsors

The Alternative Education Program/Expulsion Program — commonly known as the Alter Ed Program within the HWDSB — is one of the premier programs of its kind in Ontario. Noting that he is proud to be associated with the program, Principal Dale Pyke describes its objectives as follows:

> We are establishing an educational environment which makes student success mandatory. Our students are performing better than when they were in regular school. This we attribute to our belief in a "sense of belonging." Social/emotional programming is the key to our success. The program is research based. The key factor research has noted is students not feeling they are wanted at their regular school. Our experience tells us that they lack a sense of worth and are looking for sincere school contact. Our program is designed to re-engage students on a social/emotional level first, then provide academics in a meaningful way. We reduce the number of credits taken at one time, which relieves academic stress. Our program provides early success so they can internalize positive feelings about themselves and school.

Pyke then offers some examples.

A 19-year old who had grown up in an environment of drugs and alcohol lived in a small town outside of Hamilton. He rode his bicycle to school every day and was three credits away from graduation before being expelled. Enrolling in the Alter Ed Program (he refused to return to his home school, feeling disconnected from it), he completed his remaining credits, and after graduation, worked as student advocate for a former elementary Alter Ed student who had returned to his home school and was not meeting with success. In his five months there, the young man helped out with the Boys to Men Club and took a job in the kitchen at Jack Astor's restaurant in Ancaster, riding his bicycle to and from work (the bicycle was a graduation gift from Jack Astor's, an Alter Ed sponsor). One evening he stayed at work until 2 a.m. while waiting for an electrician to do a repair job, not arriving home (by bicycle) until 4 a.m.

Now saving his money to take the Child and Youth Worker program at Mohawk College, the young man looks back on his early educational experiences and says: "I always thought I wasn't good enough. I didn't care about myself or anyone else. When my papa died I wanted to stop living. The Alter Ed staff stood by me and refused to let me quit. They helped me understand who I was and what I could be."

The second example is a 15-year-old girl, who also had grown up amid drugs and alcohol. She entered the Alter Ed Program after becoming pregnant. During her pregnancy, she maintained a 90 percent attendance record in the program. On a Friday evening, she gave birth, and she returned to school the following Monday. Now graduated, she says, "I have found a place where adults care about me. They make me feel I have something to offer."

Finally, one student in the Alter Ed Program was an intelligent 19-year-old from a loving family. She had lost much school time because of her commitment to the national gymnastics team, on which she had often represented Canada at international competitions. She came to Alter Ed because she missed the company of her peers in school and felt that her regular secondary school did not understand her needs. In the Alter Ed Program, she completed credits in her area of study (the funeral business) through a combination of in-school courses, home study, and co-op; graduated; and is now attending college to become a mortician while still teaching gymnastics to youth. She comments that the Alter Ed Program "cared about my needs and what I wanted, not what the school wanted for me." She still visits the program occasionally to help with the Project G.O. club.

A Prince Edward Island Story of Success

Need: Re-engage youth in education

Community Connection: Local community college

A program on Prince Edward Island meets all the criteria of a program that shows CARE. It was started to focus on the needs of disengaged kids who have few if any ambitions or ideas with regard to postsecondary education or training. With the help of the school board and the Department of Education, it obtained a half-time teacher and other modest resources. During its first year, it had 16 students. Its director, Dr. Alex ("Sandy") MacDonald, reports:

> We based the program on the research literature. It is characterized by high expectations in terms of teaching and student effort. The goal is to make the learning meaningful by making the postsecondary learning environment come [alive] for the students so that the relationship between what they are learning in high school and what they will need to know after is made explicit. Also, the knowledge competencies are embedded in the skill competencies. Instead of struggling with Math for example, the Math competencies are embedded in projects so that the student has to acquire the Math skills to complete the projects. In other words we give the Math emotional resonance by tying it to something, like a project, in which the student is interested. We also embed essential skills like teamwork, interpersonal and intrapersonal functioning in the projects and the students then present their projects (in groups) at the end of each section.
>
> The students take a semester-long course which is called a career futures course. The curriculum is similar to that one would find in a well-developed career counselling program but is supplemented by emphasis on the development of essential skills. It is here that we place much emphasis on attitude and effort; we want the students to learn about themselves, about what will be asked of them when they leave high school and what they need to do to be successful in the postsecondary setting or the labour market. The second semester is spent in the Community College. They work together in teams of five on five different projects. Each project focuses on a different area of training such as trades/technology, community health, aerospace/marine, business, and information technology. The students work along with regular students and are held

to the same standard in terms of attendance and effort. At the end of each section, each team makes its presentation in front of teachers, instructors, students, staff, and parents. The results are then placed in the students' portfolio and they move on to the next project.

The results have been remarkable. Of the first sixteen students, fourteen went on to college or university; none of the students had originally planned to do so and all had been struggling in some way with the curriculum. . . .

As of 2006, the program, with permanent funding from both levels of government, was serving more than 70 students in the two English boards. It has succeeded in encouraging many students to go on to college or university. Previous teachers of the students have expressed amazement that these students are able to progress so quickly. Program participants speak highly about the program. "All in all, it has been incredibly successful."

Boys to Men

Need: To guide, support, and nurture at-risk boys

Community Connections: Community outreach worker, private funding, Toastmasters, male mentors and presenters

Boys to Men (or B2M) is a mentoring program for guiding, supporting, and nurturing at-risk boys. The program, started at Oakdale Park Middle School in Toronto in the early 1990s, has grown to more than 60 chapters in Toronto, plus six school chapters in the Hamilton-Wentworth District School Board. At the secondary school level, Boys to Men involves a way of thinking and acting that recognizes the importance of mentoring young men in a meaningful way.

The program is built upon the creation and maintenance of strong caring relationships between adult-male role models and male students. The framework used is not strict because Boys to Men does not necessarily involve a set of fixed strategies. Formalizing caring relationships through concrete action is emphasized. The actions shift and align according to the characteristics that the participants bring to the program.

The relationships that characterize Boys to Men are most effectively formed through an existing common bond. The mentor may be a teacher, coach, staff adviser, administrator, or educational assistant — all of these positions have proven to be effective. The most significant factor is that there must be a point of connection between the mentor and the mentored. Simply announcing that students should show up to Boys to Men does not work. The mentoring groups are small, and each mentor typically works with between three and five students.

It is important to recognize that a small initial group is not a sign of a weak program. Rather, a small, effective group is one cornerstone of building the momentum crucial to maintaining a solid Boys to Men program. Once a mentor has chosen the participants, teachers and parents are informed of the boys' involvement.

Typically, small homework sessions, which usually last about 45 minutes, are the first activities. Besides building the human connection, this type of start-up measure emphasizes the importance placed on academic achievement. These sessions are usually followed up by telephone calls home to update parents on their son's progress. With few exceptions, parents are thrilled that an adult is willing to invest time in their child. The homework sessions expand to exercise of leadership around the school, like helping at parents' night or at assemblies or games. The evolution continues based on the mutual understanding between mentors and mentored.

Newtonbrook Secondary School, Toronto

This secondary school has a flourishing Boys to Men program. There, Boys to Men participants go to movies, dinner, and sporting events; they also attend district-wide Boys to Men "anchor events." These events build momentum for the entire program and afford students opportunities to hear from community leaders in artistic, academic, or athletic spheres. Throughout the program, participants are monitored to measure their progress for attendance, academic achievement, and behavior at school and at home. Information is gathered anecdotally and through feedback forms.

As a Newtonbrook principal, Jim Spyropolous, reports the following:

> The bottom line for us has been bold. Each student involved in Boys to Men has shown significant progress in the areas that are measured. This is primarily due to outstanding mentors that are relentless in their pursuit of student achievement. We have been able to underline that achievement improves when students feel connected to caring adults within the school setting. The caring relationship increases accountability and creates a greater sense of responsibility. These two effects radiate when positive feedback is given to parents who are energized by the positive changes in their sons. For many of the students, Boys to Men brings renewed hope that they can be successful. This sense of hope is what drives their will to improve. The bonds that are created along the road are timeless and I am proud that many graduates of the program have become men that I now call my friends. These are the men that will in turn become better sons, fathers, husbands and, we hope, mentors. And ultimately, this is what the greatest benefit of Boys to Men is — a group of men ready to positively contribute to society.

Rockliffe Middle School

Another school that has introduced Boys to Men is Rockcliffe, also in Toronto. This program, in the words of the staff, "demonstrated that a single-sex grouping, with teachers who define themselves as mentors and programming which is tailored to meet the learning needs of boys and which exposes students to new pathways and new definitions of success is an extremely powerful tool in the battle to re-engage at-risk youth in our school system."

See Chapter 6: Teachers Who Show CARE for a profile of teacher Jim Clarke.

Besides single-gender male classes, the Rockcliffe approach encompasses the following, as outlined by Principal Kevin Battaglia and teacher Jim Clarke:

Hire mentors: The foundation of any successful program for at-risk students is the selection of staff who see themselves as mentors with instructional skills. These teachers embody the adage "You cannot teach them until you reach them." They do not ask for respect; they earn it by offering a model of integrity and character and providing every student with personal advice and learning support.

Maintain a balance between athletics and sports: BASE (Balancing Athletics and Sports in Education) is a privately funded after-school program which lengthens the school day until 6 p.m. for students who choose to take part in positive activities (homework, tutoring, games, sports, eating a nutritious snack). It gives them the opportunity to finish their schoolwork under the direction of a teacher and therefore ensures their academic success.

Overhaul curriculum: Develop an enriched "for boys" curriculum focusing on student success and career and life-choice pathways.

Battaglia and Clarke outline a typical year of Boys to Men:

Roots of Empathy is a program that has shown dramatic effect in reducing levels of aggression and bullying among schoolchildren by raising social/emotional competence and increasing empathy. The program takes place in the classrooms of children ages 3 to 14. Each class "adopts" a baby, who visits the classroom along with a parent and a trained facilitator once a month for nine months; the facilitator also visits the class before and after each baby visit. The program helps equip children with skills, information, and life lessons that they can apply to the classroom, to parenting, and to relationships throughout their lives.

Another program, Seeds of Empathy, promotes the development of empathy in children 3 to 5 years old. It is delivered in child-care centres or preschool settings.

We began the year with a three day retreat to Olympia Sports Camp to build our team through kayaking, rock climbing and with team challenges and problem-solving initiatives.

We exposed the class (more than half of whom live in fatherless homes) to the Roots of Empathy program. This program taught them about infant care and development. It challenged them to define their images of fatherhood as a boy and envision what fatherhood could mean to them as a man.

We challenged our mentees to become mentors through a partnership with George Syme Elementary School. Each of our young men was assigned to read with and mentor a grade one or two student who has been already identified as "at-risk."

We invested in resources to develop boys' literacy. The class chose their own magazine subscriptions. Novels and stories were purchased to deliver specific messages and life lessons to our young men.

We ensured that every B2M student participated in a structured Phys. Ed. Class everyday.

Politics 101 — We came to the realization that in order to become successful men, these boys needed to have a more accurate and comprehensive idea of how decisions are made within a democratic society . . . we needed to connect them to the political process. A community outreach worker helped our students develop an understanding of federal, provincial, and local politics, including a meeting with Mayor David Miller. One B2M student currently sits on the Mayor's youth leadership council.

Stock Market Math — We enriched our math programming by developing the theme of making money through the stock market. Students were taught the vocabulary and skills of researching, buying, trading, and selling stocks. They examined indicators and learned to measure the growth of their portfolio.

Chef in the Classroom — A professional chef was contracted to develop the public speaking skills of our students. As a certified "Toastmaster" and trained chef, he helped students "find their voice" through speech making and prepared with the class regular lunches [for] "dignitaries." The boys dressed up in shirts and ties and presented their speeches during a formal banquet . . .

Graffiti Art — A former El Salvadorian refugee who like many at-risk students arrived in Canada with limited skills and a poor outlook spent much of his youth creating graffiti art around our city. He developed his urban art into a successful computer graphics business and his designs are part of the marketing campaign for a large number of clothing stores, record shops etc. . . .

Urban Media Analysis — A former Bathurst Heights graduate who now runs a group home for at-risk youth offered a program aimed to developed the "critical eye" of our students as consumers. He planned a series of activities analyzing the lyrics of rap songs and the images of manhood found in advertising, movies and videos . . .

Fashion Design — A former George Harvey student shared his story of registering in Home Economics class in high school because he says "that is where the cute girls were." Once there he realized he had an aptitude and talent for fashion design and now has developed his own fashion label geared towards young men. He took our students through his creative process and shared the successes and challenges of entrepreneurship . . .

As for Rockcliffe's track record, Battaglia and Clarke note that two approaches were used to analyze the data: first, a longitudinal perspective — "How did this cohort progress behaviourally and academically between grade 6 and grade 9?" And second, a B2M versus Rockcliffe comparison — "How did this cohort compare to the average male Rockcliffe student?"

On the first point, it was determined that more than one-half of the B2M students were prone to arriving late or skipping classes in their previous academic year. Of them, 93 percent reduced their number of late arrivals or absences. Twenty students were transferred from Grade 6 to 7 or from Grade 7 to 8. In regular programming, 17 percent of the students were consistently promoted. After a year in B2M, 83 percent met all applicable requirements for promotion from Grade 8 to 9. Of the students who had five or more office referrals in Grade 7, 100 percent had fewer office referrals in Grade 8. Of students who had been suspended two or more times in Grade 7, 100 percent had fewer suspensions in Grade 8.

On the second point, 71 percent of the B2M cohort had a lower rate of absenteeism than the Rockcliffe male average, and 75 percent of them had a lower rate of lateness than the Rockcliffe male average. Also, 63 percent of the B2M cohort had a higher overall yearly "grade" than the average Rockcliffe male (a strong indicator of success given that more than one-half of the class had required remedial/informal special education support in prior years); 75 percent of the B2M cohort had no office referrals; and 88 percent had no suspensions.

In conclusion, Battaglia and Clarke assert that "every student, every parent and every teacher surveyed in our end-of-year assessment returned positive feedback for this program and recommended its continuation and development. They listed a long series of positive impacts on themselves, their families and their classrooms."

B2M at Downsview Public School

What convinced Principal André Patterson of the need for a mentorship program at his elementary school for Kindergarten to Grade 5 students was a conversation with a trustee. The trustee said that of the almost 50 expulsion hearings he had been involved with, all of the students had had evidence of discipline problems dating back to elementary school "and very little was done to intervene."

Patterson, already familiar with B2M, decided that his leadership would begin and end with a mentorship philosophy. First, he identified the need for mentorship largely through playground observation and specific boys who would benefit; then, he ensured that he was seen as a welcoming presence and periodically had informal, motivating talks with certain boys. The Boys Book Club got underway and gained momentum through the school district. Students from a neighbouring high school became mentors for a homework club.

Patterson leads by example. He writes: "The opportunity to play organized sports at the elementary school level is almost non-existent; I faced the same situation at my elementary school. Many times leading by example is the only way to lead an initiative. I ran a multi-sports club once a week after school. By the second year, we had a regular intramural program at lunch, boys and girls varsity soccer, basketball, and a co-ed volleyball team. These activities were accessible to all. However, one important message was always communicated — being on the team was a privilege not a right."

As evidence of B2M's success, some mentored students have gone on to take part in peer mediation groups, Student Council, and a Future Possibilities club. Patterson reflects on his initiative: "I began with the expectation that all children will succeed in school, then focused on the school's role in providing meaningful programs and resources for all students, then built on students' strengths. I believe I am able to make a difference for students before they end up in an expulsion hearing wondering where it all went wrong." The principal says that if schools are to ensure success, "they need to focus on improving the quality of the school experience, rather than trying to fix the character of the student."

CHOICES Youth Program, Winnipeg

Need: To promote positive life skills and choices to at-risk youth

Community Connections: Manitoba Department of Justice, volunteer university students

The CHOICES youth program has been reaching out to and connecting with at-risk youth for more than 10 years in Manitoba. It is a unique, award-winning, and comprehensive program that gives youth the skills they need to make healthy choices in their lives. The program is funded by the Manitoba government, through the Department of Justice, is supported by several community partnerships, and has 120 students enrolled in six schools in the Winnipeg School Division.

The overall goal of CHOICES is to build resilience in youth. The Circle of Courage model (Brendtro, Brokenleg, and Bockern 1990) serves as its guiding philosophy. Its concepts of Belonging, Mastery, Independence, and Generosity are integrated throughout all facets of CHOICES.

Throughout the year, the program motto "Be Respectful, Be Safe and Be Responsible" is taught and reinforced.

Students participating in CHOICES are expected to learn that they have a choice in the decisions they make, that they can make positive lifestyle choices, and that logical consequences follow their actions. The program has several objectives: enhanced self-esteem, sense of personal worth and usefulness; positive coping skills and behaviors; understanding of the need for higher education; positive interpersonal relationships; and academic and employment skills. As staff report, it connects with youth (Grades 6 to 8) via five components:

- *Classroom*: The classroom facilitator (a Justice employee) meets with each of the school groups once in a 6 day cycle. Building a sense of belonging is the first challenge within the group. Classroom curriculum focuses on developing social skills to build resiliency and covers topics such as communication, anger management, gang resistance, substance-abuse prevention, and conflict mediation. There is a school staff member who acts as a CHOICES contact in each school.
- *Mentor*: The evening mentor program brings youth and role models (volunteer university students) together one evening a week for fun learning activities, sport and field trips. The purpose of this component is to provide emotional support to attend school and community activities. It also reinforces and develops mastery of skills taught in the classroom program. The volunteer mentors become caring and significant adults in the lives of the youth.
- *Follow up*: The follow up club is the component where each young person is connected to a positive activity of their choice within the community. Choices may include sport, music, or the arts. Students demonstrate generosity through participation in volunteer activities.
- *Family*: Family nights, which happen once a month, are an opportunity for the youth and their family to build connections through social activities. The families are transported by bus to the activity and back to their schools. Examples of outings are hockey and baseball games, roller skating, or bowling. Parents also receive a monthly newsletter (with parenting tips and program updates) and are encouraged to call the program coordinator as needed.
- *Wilderness*: The wilderness program provides 3 outings throughout the year (1/2 day wall climbing and team building, an overnight winter camp, and a 3 day canoe or hiking trip). This component reinforces and tests the skills youth learn in the classroom and evening program in real-life settings and fosters independence.

Staff, in 2006, stated that "over the years we have witnessed some remarkable and gratifying changes in many of the young people who graduate from CHOICES. A follow up evaluation of the program showed that youth completing CHOICES were 66% less likely to be involved with the law."

Staff identified several positive examples. One person, Jessica, had to deal with the death of her mother during her year in CHOICES. She and the aunt with whom she was living said that CHOICES helped get them through a terrible time. Another student, formerly in the CHOICES program, offered to be a mentor while working as an education assistant in a CHOICES school. She then went on to train in the Winnipeg police academy. Yet another, Matt, who entered the armed forces after his time in CHOICES, frequently says to others: "Know your role and be respectful."

NYA WEH, Sir John A. Macdonald Secondary School, Hamilton

Needs: To enable Aboriginal students to learn about their culture and how to live healthy lives

Community Connections: Aboriginal elder, the broader Aboriginal community, Health Clinic, Hamilton Community Foundation, community volunteers

NYA WEH (Native Youth Advancement With Education Hamilton) endeavors to provide a "culturally based educational and personal support program for Aboriginal youth" within Hamilton's secondary school environment. It aims to offer all of the supports necessary for Aboriginal students to succeed at school and ultimately attain their secondary school diplomas. The program recognizes that intertwining the Western and Traditional streams of education is essential if Aboriginal youth are to enjoy success in mainstream society. As its Web site puts it: "Both systems are viewed as necessary assets to advance as healthy individuals, Communities and Nations."

Students come to a dedicated resource room where youth advisers are based. The NYA WEH room "offers a culturally oriented environment where Aboriginal students are able to feel welcomed and comfortable." It includes computers with Internet access, a library with significant Aboriginal content, and stationery supplies. Aboriginal youth advisers provide academic support, so that students complete assignments and homework. They offer personal or social guidance, provide access to tutors, and also advocate on behalf of students when any issues arise with school staff or peers.

The program has components related to culture, personal development, nutrition, and employment.

In the Aboriginal Leadership Workshop, a life skills instructor and a traditional elder coach the students in building personal capacity through culture and education. "This workshop teaches students the ability to recognize and create opportunities that will benefit their growth and development."

In Traditional Drum and Dance, students can learn contemporary and traditional Pow Wow songs and traditional dance. Each art form has its own time slot after school on separate days. Since the workshop is inclusive of both genders, females have an opportunity to learn hand drum songs and Pow Wow dances traditionally specific to women. As part of the program, participants can design and construct their own regalia.

The Aboriginal Nutrition Program, coordinated with the Aboriginal Health Clinic, "is based on participation and youth friendly presentations that encourage healthy eating alternatives while highlighting the negative health impacts of foods popular within youth circles." This program aims to address some of the ailments common in Aboriginal communities: these include diabetes and obesity.

Breakfast and lunch programs are offered daily. Students can drop in to the NYA WEH room, on the second floor of Sir John A. Macdonald, for breakfast, at designated break times, and at lunchtime. Nutritional snacks and meal options are available to them. A parent of a graduated NYA WEH student volunteers her time a few days a week to prepare hot breakfasts and lunches for the students.

NYA WEH has experienced great growth since it began with six students at the outset of 2003 — within a month it had expanded to 35 students. Enrolment then increased to 52 in 2004–2005, and to 63 in 2005–2006. By the end of phase 1, the program was serving 90 youth.

The word "nya:weh" means thank you in Mohawk.

Triangle of Hope

Need: To foster interaction between various school communities; to provide financial support for enrichment programs

Community Connection: Stephen Leacock Foundation for Children

Three Triangles of Hope

Public schools
Derrydown Public School (Jane and Finch community)
Rose Avenue Public School (St. James community)
Woburn Junior Public School (Scarborough)
Independent schools
Crescent School, North York
Havergal School, north Toronto
Branksome Hall, midtown Toronto
South African schools
Get Ahead Project School, Whittlesea, Eastern Cape
Get Ahead Project School, Queenstown, Eastern Cape
Get Ahead Project College, Queenstown, Eastern Cape

Branksome Hall is a member of the Triangle of Hope, founded by restaurateur and philanthropist, Peter Oliver, chair of the Stephen Leacock Foundation for Children. The Triangle of Hope project partners a Toronto independent school with a Toronto inner-city school and a school in South Africa's Eastern Cape. Branksome's local partner in the Triangle of Hope is Rose Avenue Public School, and the Toronto schools' South African partner is the Get Ahead Project School in Queenstown. Together, they work to increase intercultural understanding and provide opportunities for student learning, service, and friendship. At time of writing, there were three Triangles of Hope operating in Toronto.

The Triangle of Hope project began at Branksome in 2004, and each year since then, some senior Branksome students and faculty have travelled to South Africa. The Branksome students help at the Queenstown Get Ahead Project School, running a number of projects with the students and staff. Branksome students lead classes and interact with student groups while the South African and Canadian teachers share curriculum initiatives.

As part of their partnership with the local school, groups of Branksome Hall students go weekly to Rose Avenue Public School to run the after-school Homework Club, the JUMP Math Tutoring program, and the Rose Avenue Band. Each summer, 35 Grades 4 and 5 students from Rose Avenue come to a month-long Literacy Camp at Branksome Hall, funded by the Leacock Foundation. Branksome students volunteer at Literacy Camp and faculty from Branksome assist in running the camp.

In general, the Stephen Leacock Foundation for Children goes where the need is greatest and pursues its goals through strategic partnerships. The foundation has refined its giving strategy through the Triangle of Hope. The program provides financial support for curriculum and school-community enrichment programs for vulnerable school-aged children both in Canada and in the developing world.

As described above, this unique program unites three schools from two countries: Canada and South Africa. One Canadian school is inner-city; the other is privileged (private). The three-way voluntary partnership provides both tangible and intangible benefits to each school. Goals of the program are to help students from all ages and walks of life to interact in a meaningful way, to understand one another, to break down the various geographic, cultural, and economic barriers that might exist between them, and to provide financial support for the disadvantaged schools. In the case of Canada, the inner-city schools are weakened by diminishing public school board budgets; in the case of the developing world, the schools lack sufficient government support of public education and benefit from "bricks and mortar" projects.

Educators associated with the Triangle of Hope program report that the financial support they receive from the Stephen Leacock Foundation for Children is fostering a renewed sense of hope in their disadvantaged school communities. At the same time, at privileged schools, student volunteers can learn and grow through outreach and volunteerism on a local and a global scale. Efforts to build respectful, cooperative relationships among parents, families, teachers, and school administrators help family members feel more capable of contributing to their child's education and more connected to their child's school.

The Youth Pathways and Transitions Program, Halifax

Need: To address the needs of students suspended from school, including facilitating full-time return to their home schools

Community Connections: Access to a social worker and a psychologist

Matthew didn't like school much. Frustrated and angry, the youth would often get into fights with his fellow students. On more than one occasion, his fighting got him suspended. Finally, his repeated behavioral problems landed him a long-term suspension.

In the past, such a youth would have been sent home for the duration of his suspension. He would have received homework packages from the school to keep up with his work, and he may have had access to services such as tutoring and behavioral programs — he would have been away from school for a long time.

Thanks to the Youth Pathways and Transitions program, that did not happen to Matthew. Matthew was able to work on his behavioral issues in a school environment. While he didn't like all aspects of school, he returned to class, focused on learning and "getting his work done." He attended class in the Youth Pathways and Transitions program (YPT) at St. Patrick's High School (now called the Quinpool Education Centre) in Halifax.

YPT was established in 2004 in response to a school board motion, put forward by Douglas Sparks, an African Canadian, to develop a plan of action to address the needs of students suspended from schools.

Sparks was concerned with students falling through the cracks. "Too many of our students, regardless of their background or race, do not find success in the traditional classroom setting," he says. "It's imperative for us to look at alternative programs and methods of delivery as a means of accommodating their needs."

Noreen Stymest is the department head for YPT. She oversees four teachers and ideally about 18 students (numbers have gone above 40) at any one time. The program is open to all students in Grades 7 through 12 in the Halifax Regional School Board, and students arrive throughout the year, usually after a referral from their home school.

"Typically students spend between 10 to 12 weeks with us and then transition back to their school," says Stymest. "Our goal is to respond to their academic needs and provide them with the necessary support to positively address their past problems."

The support is provided in a number of ways.

To begin with, the low pupil–teacher ratio gives teachers plenty of time with each student. This helps build trust — not a small thing when many of the students experiencing trouble feel that no one at school is on their side or understands their problems.

Another significant support is access to a social worker and a psychologist. "Students are able to receive individual counselling and then have immediate opportunities to build or improve those skills in a social setting within a small group," says Stymest.

Relationships between teachers and students are close and collaborative. At lunchtime, for example, students and staff are encouraged to stay in the lunchroom to socialize, play board games, listen to music, or talk. These connections, so simple yet important, help the students when it comes time for them to begin the transition back to their home school. The transition begins slowly — usually one or two days per week — and builds up to full time. The goal is to sustain their return.

"Saying goodbye is a time to celebrate," says Stymest. "Seeing positive change regardless of how incremental makes working here very rewarding." About 80 percent of students successfully make the transition.

City Centre Education Project, Edmonton

Need: To enable inner-city school students to experience academic success

Community Connections: Various business and agency partnerships

The goal of the Edmonton Public Schools' City Centre Education Project (CCEP) is to achieve superb academic results from all students. The program, created by the Board of Trustees in April 2001, is founded on three pillars: "(a) support for the critical work of teaching and learning that goes on in the classroom; (b) interagency and business partnerships; and (c) organization as a multi-campus model." Its director has described the project as "a family of seven inner city schools that work collaboratively to maximize the resources they need to meet the needs of the students in their unique communities."

The Edmonton trustees recognized that significant changes had to be made if all inner-city students were to graduate from Grade 12. They undertook to transform programming for students from Junior Kindergarten to Grade 9. By 2005, CCEP had a coordinator and 150 staff serving about 1700 students with needs ranging from behavior to literacy to schizophrenia.

Through this reconfiguration of the city centre schools, school administrators are able to collectively pool their many resources, while still maintaining their distinctiveness. This innovative model also means that children attending a CCEP school have access to enriched programming opportunities that focus on improving literacy and numeracy skills — priorities adopted by the board and measured by Edmonton Public Schools' reading and writing standardized tests, CCEP performance based assessments and the province of Alberta standardized achievement tests.

The Board's commitment to improving student learning has meant that CCEP schools benefit from many programs and services. These include full-day Kindergarten, balanced literacy programming, Reading Recovery, lots of professional development, the presence of teacher-librarians, enrichment programming for gifted children, specialist teachers for core and enrichment courses, mentors to support the academic and social development of students; a wide range of extra-curricular activities (e.g., band, choir, tutorials, active living program, young chefs), field-trip experiences aligned with curriculum, school-sponsored family events and parent information sessions, transportation for students to have access to programming not in their "home" school, and morning snack. There is also regular access to a school nurse (1.5 days per week), a family therapist, and an Aboriginal youth worker for Junior High school students in government care. Three of the schools offer half-day, play-based, academically focused programming for children 3.5 to 4.5 years old.

Beyond that, parents play advisory roles at three school levels. Each of the seven schools has a parent advisory council, there is a CCEP parent advisory council with representation from all seven schools, and at the district level, a strong "key communicators" group serves.

To further enhance student learning, the Board has developed numerous partnerships with agencies in the local community. Among these groups are Big Brothers and Big Sisters Society of Edmonton & Area, the YMCA, Capital Health, City of Edmonton's Community Services, Edmonton Police Service, the Family Centre, and more. The Edmonton Community Foundation is also a partner.

There are other major partners. These include the provincial Department of Children's Services; Region 6 Child and Family Services; Health Canada; Roots of Empathy, Grant McEwan College; Girl Guides of Canada; Metro College Dance and Cool School program; John Janzen Nature Centre; AADAC (Alberta Alcohol and Drug Abuse Commission); a researcher; and an anonymous donor. These partnerships go beyond cash donations; the partners directly offer learning opportunities and engage with individual students.

One strong example of the value of working collaboratively with the community is the success of the Preventing Type 2 Diabetes Among Inner City School-Aged Children project. Called the Healthy Eating, Active Living Initiative, this project supports and celebrates healthy choices by students at any of the seven CCEP schools.

The director of CCEP has given credit for the success of the program in this way:

> The strength of CCEP is that the model was based on the needs and strengths of the community in which it is situated, and built on the unconditional support from the Board of Trustees whose number one priority is to ensure that students receive the best possible education and the commitment of students, families, district staff members and community members to the project.

Since this program was implemented during 2000–2001, it has earned parental praise. It has attracted an improved percentage of students, and parents have expressed high levels of satisfaction when it comes to children's achievement, attitudes towards school, and behavior.

Program Benefits as Identified by Staff, Students, Parents, and Community Partners

The following represents qualitative data gathered by Prof. Jose L. da Costa from the Department of Educational Policy Studies at the University of Alberta.

- CCEP has improved student learning;
- CCEP has increased access to resources and programs for students;
- CCEP has increased staff's understanding of what is required to promote success for students in the city centre;
- CCEP has enabled teachers to focus on instruction and created shared leadership;
- CCEP has increased staff collaboration and access to colleagues' expertise;
- CCEP has created a preventative approach by helping address students' learning needs more immediately;
- CCEP has increased the professional development available to staff;
- CCEP has increased parental involvement and support to parents;
- CCEP has increased the willingness to take risks and has created a new way of working for all staff and community partners involved; and
- CCEP has provided new ways of working with other organizations to meet the needs of students and families.

Best Start Strategy, Ministry of Children and Youth Services, Ontario

Need: To meet the various growth and development needs of children and youth through integrated, community-responsive services

Community Connections: All provincial ministries that have some connection to children and youth

The Best Start Strategy is the centrepiece program of the Ministry of Children and Youth Services (MCYS), which the Ontario government created in 2003. The role of the ministry is to build a more seamless and rational system of services for children and youth. It is to set the government's policy agenda for children and youth; lead the implementation of the Best Start Strategy; influence other ministries to assess their policies and programs for impact on children and youth; manage the system of children's services; and deliver services directly.

Through the MCYS, all children and youth programs will be brought together into an integrated system of services for young people up to the age of 18. Some government-funded children's programs — such as those managed by the ministries of Community and Social Services, Health and Long-Term Care, and Community Safety and Correctional Services — have been transferred to the MCYS. Some services have also been transferred to the MCYS, but they continue to be delivered through existing agencies and organizations, such as public health units, children's aid societies, Early Years Centres, and daycare centres. The difference is that the planning and funding for those services are now integrated. Communities across the province are thereby encouraged to take a more integrated approach to serving children and families.

Other programs for children and youth are still delivered by the original ministries, including Education, Citizenship and Immigration, Culture, and Tourism. However, the MCYS is responsible for working closely with them and with other community partners to plan and coordinate services.

The threefold goal is to give children the best possible start in life, to prepare youth to become productive adults, and to make it easier for families to get the services they need at all stages of a child's development.

The Best Start Strategy is distinct from other initiatives in that it

- responds to the clear message that communities need more integrated accessible services for young children and families;
- focuses on meeting the needs of children and families by strengthening, enhancing, building on, and integrating existing programs and services;
- asks all existing organizations that provide services for children from birth to age six — regardless of which ministry funds them — to share their expertise and plan together; and
- is community driven in that the ways in which services are delivered are determined by the participating communities based on their specific needs and strengths.

Because Best Start is government guided, but community driven, it will look different in various communities — for example, rural, urban, francophone, and Aboriginal. It is too early to formally assess the program's effectiveness, but it seems to be having a positive impact.

Although it's true that today's young people are struggling with a multitude of risk factors, the majority of those I have met are determined to make better lives for themselves. The major causes of students leaving school are their disconnection and disengagement with the school culture and school community, rather than their personal and family circumstances. Kids need to feel that the system cares about them. We need to pay attention to them so that they know they are valued.

Many of the people in the programs identified in this chapter took a special interest in those students not succeeding. Typically, each student was paired with a caring adult — a teacher, a guidance counsellor, or an administrator — who personally worked with and provided advice to the student.

To me, the challenge for system leaders is clear: to institutionalize the connection between a caring adult in the school and those students who are struggling in a variety of ways and across a variety of dimensions — academically, socially, and more. It is clearly the case that a teach-as-I-was-taught approach misses many students. We know that students approach learning differently. While research supports the use of learning style and intelligence preference theories in the classroom and points to the importance of addressing gender and culture-based approaches to learning, experience tells me that relationships matter most!

CHAPTER 6

Teachers Who Show CARE

The demands placed upon educators seem unrelenting. I, for one, marvel and take great pride in the work they do every day with kids, the way they balance innumerable competing concerns and still find a way to connect to kids. Their work is truly heroic.

All teaching and learning staff work hard at what they do, yet must sometimes feel as if they are taken for granted. So, before I proceed any further, let me stop just for a moment to say "thank you." Educators are remarkable people.

How should we think about all the issues we face? What matters most? Let me suggest that the holistic development of students remains the primary reason we are here.

Kids today have the language of independence — they act and talk and look as if they are almost adults, but inside, as we all know, they are still children, looking to us for guidance even as they claim to reject it, craving our boundary-setting even as they claim they don't need it.

We owe it to kids to clearly communicate what we expect them to learn and do. Somewhat similarly, as adults, we would expect no less from our employers. Kids need to know that the grown-ups have thought about their educational experience and planned it in a way that connects past, present, and future: This is the road map. On any journey, whether it takes four days in a car or 13 years in school, people need to know where they have come from and where they are going.

My faith in education is renewed daily by schools that provide an oasis of hope through teachers who consistently create educational magic in their classrooms, who move and motivate their students to learn. But beyond recognizing magic at work, what makes a great teacher? I have identified 11 characteristics.

1. Passion for teaching: As French philosopher Denis Diderot said, "Only passions, great passions, can elevate the soul to do great things."
2. Love of your subject: Great teachers also love to share that love with their students.
3. Love of kids: It's not enough for teachers to talk about how they love and know about their subjects — they need to mention the kids, too.
4. Understanding the role of school in a child's life: Some of the best teaching can happen on basketball courts, in halls after class, in a drama studio, and so on — the best teachers know

that they are teachers for much more than the time spent in the classroom.

5. A willingness to change: Schools should be as transformative for teachers as they are supposed to be for students.
6. A work ethic by which you give all that you can give: The overwhelming majority of the teachers I've met put in hours well above and beyond the contract.
7. A willingness to reflect: Teaching requires a willingness to cast a critical eye on personal teaching practice, pedagogy, and self — and it can be brutal.
8. Organization: Students should know what they are going to learn and what is expected of them while their teachers have both structure and spontaneity.
9. Enough humility to remember that you can learn from your students: If teachers cannot understand that a 16-year-old can tell them something they do not know, then they shouldn't teach, at least not high school.
10. A willingness to work collaboratively: Although some great teachers shut the doors to their classrooms and do what they want, that sometimes sends a strange message to kids; even when a school community is flawed, a great teacher should be part of it and work to make it better.
11. Understanding that being a "great teacher" is a journey, not a destination

In short, great teachers provide students with inspiration and encouragement above and beyond customary expectations. They clearly demonstrate positive spirit, intelligence, generosity, and high moral purpose in their professional endeavors. They show initiative, tenacity, and unselfishness in pursuit of teaching excellence.

Over the years I have met many teachers who fit the above description. In this chapter, I write about only seven of them, all of whom share in abundance the qualities of teachers who show CARE: who care, accept, respect, and engage.

Teaching beyond the Classroom

For 25 years, Bob Maydo has taught at-risk students in some of Toronto's most challenging communities. His basic philosophy? "If I can't reach them, I cannot teach them." Many students have "found" themselves as a result of Maydo's care and concern. He treats each student with respect. Chosen as Ontario's Teacher of the Year in 1986, he is totally committed to helping students academically and personally, in or out of school.

"My teaching goes beyond the classroom," he says. "If kids don't have their personal lives together, everything is that much harder. Over the years I have had the privilege to work with kids who epitomize resiliency. The least I can do is help."

At break, Maydo can be seen in the halls, greeting kids with "high-fives" and pats on the back. No matter where he is, this phenomenon happens. Whenever he sees one of his students, there is the usual warm greeting. Bonds of respect and care unite Maydo and his students.

Beyond being an excellent teacher, Maydo has established himself as one of the most successful high-school basketball coaches in Canada. He recognizes sports as an activity that provides opportunities for character building and may have a critical effect in socializing youth. Through sports participation, he believes, students learn not only how to play a specific sport, but also how to play the game of life.

A Friend Girls Can Count On

"Educational change depends on what teachers do and think — it's as simple and as complex as that."

— Michael Fullan with Suzanne Steigelbauer

Another model teacher is Karlene Ebanks, who founded the Gyrlfryndz at Rockcliffe Middle School in Toronto. There, she provides opportunities for at-risk teenaged girls to expand their horizons. She empowers these girls to take control over their bodies and their futures. From organizing dance classes and sexual empowerment seminars to taking her "gyrlz" to Toronto Raptors games or theatre shows, Ebanks shows herself to be a friend that the girls can count on. (Activities are funded through school initiatives and donations.) She is also a teacher who demonstrates to her students how they can build bridges to a promising future.

Providing a Strong Base for Boys

Jim Clarke also goes above and beyond the call of duty. In 2004–2005, he initiated the program Balancing Academics and Sports in Education (BASE) at Rockcliffe Middle School in Toronto. After a full day of teaching his all-boys Boys to Men Grade 8 class, he spends three more hours mentoring a broader range of male students and providing them with positive options. Every school day, students in the BASE program play in a games room (featuring air hockey, football, Xbox, Ping-Pong, and so forth) for an hour, do homework for an hour, and then play structured games in the gym for an hour. The boys receive healthy snacks and peer tutoring. Other teachers regularly report that Clarke's BASE students do better in the classroom because of his positive message and willingness to take responsibility for ensuring that all his students learn. Jim Clarke is a teacher who cares.

Office administrators can show CARE, too. While I was director of education for Hamilton-Wentworth, Heidi Snelling shared with me her passion for yoga. She convinced me that yoga helps students develop the focus and concentration skills they need to enhance learning and work independently despite distractions. Yoga can also help students manage the symptoms of ADHD, and process and handle their emotions so as to diffuse anger and stress. A pilot program exploring yoga and student achievement has resulted.

Offering Tickets to Success

Consider, too, Steve Lashbrook and Sharon Backman, who joined the Music Department of Toronto's Central Technical School in 1996.

Lashbrook and Backman had a vision of expanding the vocal program, adding courses in drama and guitar, and building a high-tech recording studio to facilitate a course in songwriting and recording. The studio now produces commercial quality CDs at the very good rate of one per year. The music, a fusion of rock, jazz, hip hop, rap, and rhythm and blues, addresses the issues and emotions that young people deal with as they become adults.

Many of these young recording artists are not average teenagers. The school's diverse, urban population includes low-income, at-risk students from across the city. Many are from single-parent homes or are living in poverty, and some have spent time in shelters for the homeless or been involved in or affected by crime.

"More than 50 percent of the students we work with come from exceptional circumstances," Lashbrook says, relating the story of one student who was living in a shelter and yet advanced to the top 30 on the television program *Canadian Idol*. He further notes that, by teaching students to play instruments, craft songs, develop their voices, and use computers and other modern tools to compose and record music, the program offers a practical way for students to develop the skills and confidence they need to achieve success.

A Natural in the Classroom

My six-year-old son Jake insisted that I acknowledge his Kindergarten teacher, Aviva Dunsiger, as "an awesome teacher — because she cares." What he likes especially is that even before he started Kindergarten with her, she would make weekly visits to the daycare to get to know him and other incoming students. By the time he entered her classroom in September, she knew that he was interested in dinosaurs and animals — and so they were a part of the classroom. He was impressed.

For my part, I have come to realize that some people are naturals in the classroom, and Dunsiger is one of them. She can easily engage her students and she has a dynamic classroom presence. She reveals an innate understanding of how to do the delicate dance that will engage her young charges.

Building Strong Relationships

Totally dedicated as a teacher, unbelievably patient, compassionate to a fault; does not accept failure in any student; gives of his time, talent, and encouragement. Takes a real personal interest in students, especially those most in need. A teacher, a mentor, a Father *figure, and a friend . . .*

Of course, he shared his knowledge of the subject matter. But the encouragement to learn was what made the difference — he motivated students to learn far beyond the classroom.

Meet Tim Skinner, one of the greatest teachers I have known. His greatness has come from his strong relationships with his students and his ability to care about them as people. During his career, now based at Emery Collegiate in Toronto, he has never missed a teachable moment and has always been willing to give the shirt off his back — literally — to support his students. He is warm, accessible, enthusiastic, and damn funny! Often, he has stayed after school to make himself available to students and parents who needed him.

Skinner also has taken parental involvement to a whole new level. He routinely has visited parents at home, at work, or in a coffee shop at almost any time of the day. Parents have trusted him so much that they

Teachers make a difference not only in what their students learn about content, but in what they learn about life!

have asked him to be their children's surrogate parent. His influence on students, staff, and community is felt immediately, and his impact remains legendary.

Keeping the Beat with Social Justice

Teacher Barry Smith believes that educators must use their course work to help students understand the world and to empower them to remedy injustices. Teachers must also serve as role models in pursuing social justice.

Smith first came to this conclusion after a Students for Political Action symposium in 2002. He found that one non-governmental agency, War Child Canada, captured students' imaginations. Wanting to do something about children in war-affected countries, students took part in Keep the Beat, a music marathon fundraiser that many North American schools support.

"In our first year of music and message we raised just over $5,000! The most ever!" he wrote. "Five years later we had cumulatively raised $77,500 with our community — the most War Child had ever seen!"

Once Smith learned that War Child was directing the funds raised by the school to rebuild a school in the Democratic Republic of Congo, the scene of brutal fighting, he wanted to go there. In early 2008, he got that chance when Dr. Samantha Nutt, founder and director of War Child Canada, invited him to go on a fact-finding mission to East Congo. As he put it: "The journey was life-changing. Though I witnessed the most crushing poverty and devastation from war I have ever seen, I was more conscious of the hope and optimism in everyone I met. I visited the school in Makabola and touched the sign — and wept."

During his visit, he met a teacher who had lost his family in the massacre that had befallen the village when the original school was destroyed. The teacher told him "Education is the only way my country will heal itself. It is the only thing we have that can give the children hope to make a better Congo. I teach here because it *will* make a difference for my future and theirs [the students']."

Back home in Hamilton, Ontario, Smith worked with like-minded educators to share the tenets of social justice education and find ways to make the curriculum more meaningful. "I shared with my colleagues a message from a recent Environics poll that 90% of students showed a keen interest in the world around them and named teachers as their number one source for information and inspiration in this pursuit."

A Social Justice Network, a group of teachers committed to the idea that students could build character through social justice education, evolved. The network has held at least three Social Justice Fairs, the first bringing together more than 300 students and more than 30 non-governmental organizations to share work being done in schools and around the world. Among many initiatives, students have sent a mural of hope, petitions, and a Student Declaration of commitment to the United Nations. The network has also produced teacher workshops and an entire social justice program for senior students; it is moving towards a film festival aligned to UN goals.

"As a society becomes more enlightened, it realizes that it is responsible not to transmit and conserve the whole of its existing achievements, but only such as make for a better future society. The school is the chief agency for the accomplishment of this end."

— John Dewey

Another champion for social justice education is Beth Carey. Perhaps her greatest contribution is coordinating Hamilton's Me to We Day at Hamilton Place, where more than 2000 students from at least 80 schools gathered for a high energy day. After students heard philanthropists Craig and Marc Kielburger and entertainment by socially conscious acts like Liam Titcomb and Sol Guy, they left empowered and excited about doing their part to make a positive difference.

"Social justice as a lens of learning has become more robust in me through my journey to Congo and Uganda," reports Smith. "The experience taught me that my skills as an educator have to be put to work to inspire. I have to believe that students need not merely inherit a world they are given when they have the opportunity to *craft* the world they want. When educators care enough to inspire through education as a means of revitalizing Congo — it is incumbent upon *all* educators to learn from that action!"

A Big Difference

Teachers have an astounding ability to make a difference in the world. Passing knowledge on to students is just a part of what the finest teachers do — the best are those who influence their students' social and emotional development as well as their self-confidence. They may wear the hat of instructor, but they also are counselors, mentors, servants, coaches, and administrators. Perhaps most important, they inspire. They teach because it matters. They touch the future. The influence of the great ones extends beyond the confines of the classroom to affect the rest of students' lives.

Teachers' own beliefs and attitudes play a role in their effectiveness. When teachers feel that they are making a difference and are supported by their principals and community, their motivation to teach increases, and their students' results improve, as well. Teaching is not occurring unless learning is taking place. Good teachers know this. Children also realize this. Students who go home full of stories about what they learned that day probably experienced teaching by a good teacher.

Identifying a good teacher is easy, but creating and promoting a school *full* of good teachers should be the goal of our educational system. A place to start is in nurturing new teachers. School administrators and boards need to make a teacher's transition into the classroom safe and pleasant. Teachers need to be supported through well-thought-out professional development. They need trained mentors with whom they can consult and reflect. Finally, all of us must recognize that teachers *do* make a difference in a child's learning — a big difference.

When a new teacher comes to the school, I tell them, "If you went into teaching to make a difference, I welcome you. But with these kids, you won't *make* a difference: You will *be* the difference."

Staff must believe in their individual and collective capacities to bring about change that benefits students.

110

Conclusion: Towards Realizing a Common Vision

As an educator for more than 20 years, I can tell you that schools that show CARE have ignited the flame of hope and promise that will light the way to a nation in which every child will have access to a great public school education. In the course of my visits to numerous schools across Canada, I have been impressed by the staffs' recognition that, beyond being places of formal learning for their students, schools are community assets: assets that have the potential to improve the lives of community members. These schools offer children, youth, and families opportunities to contribute to their communities and build the kinds of skills, values, and attitudes necessary for lifelong success. From them, I have learned the six truths of schools that show CARE.

Truth 1: The attitude will determine the altitude.

In schools with better learning results for all students, school leaders believe that they can make a difference in the lives of all children. They envision a better future for students and they are clear about (1) how they need to change and (2) how the school needs to change in order to make the vision real.

They develop SMART goals in collaboration with staff, students, and community. These can be presented through the following questions.

Specific and **S**trategic — Have you articulated precisely what you want to achieve, and have priorities been strategically selected based on a comprehensive needs assessment?
Measurable — Are you able to assess or measure your progress?
Attainable — Is the goal within your reach and within your control? Are targets ambitious yet attainable?
Results-based — Have you established base-line data and targets of where you want to end up?
Time-bound — What is the deadline for reaching your goal?

The most important variable pertaining to attitude is what teachers *do*, not what they know. What they should strive to do is summed up in these five change-focused points:

- We must improve instructional practice through professional development in learning communities.
- We must focus on the change we need and the research supporting the change.

111

- We must then hold all educators accountable for the change.
- We must support all educators in their efforts to change.
- We must believe that schools can change and can make a difference.

The achievement gap is ultimately vulnerable to the greatness inherent in all children and to the power of talented, hard-working adults of vision who have a sense of urgency in addressing it.

Truth 2: Successful schools teach all students more.

In high-achieving schools, challenging academic content has become standard in every classroom at every grade. All students receive access to rigorous academic coursework. Content has been upgraded and students are being challenged to learn new skills.

There is a shared understanding that we are preparing our students to be productive citizens in a global community, who will be selling to and buying from the world; working for international companies; managing employees from other countries and cultures; competing with people on the other side of the world for jobs and markets; working with people all over the world in joint ventures and global work teams; and solving global problems, such as AIDS, environmental issues, and conflicts.

Depth is more critical than breadth. Teachers in schools that show CARE do not teach everything; however, they teach the most important things exceptionally well. They also use data to identify and prioritize the key standards that must be taught exceptionally well.

Truth 3: Assessment drives instruction.

If you don't know that something has been learned, then you don't know whether it has been taught. Assessment *for* learning is the catalyst for school improvement.

In schools that show CARE, educators use frequent interim assessments to gauge student progress towards learning key content. Great teachers see assessments more as starting blocks than as finish lines. They use results to improve instruction immediately. Assessment information is mined for clues about how to improve student understanding of key learning objectives. Leaders display data that help educators understand how teaching can improve.

In schools that show CARE, assessment results help determine professional learning needs. As professional development initiatives are implemented, assessment results are used to gauge the effectiveness of those efforts.

Truth 4: Students learn when taught in ways that help them learn.

In schools that show CARE, educators are continuously learning how to adapt instruction in ways that help students learn well. Educators learn to instruct in ways that are responsive to the learning strengths, backgrounds, cultures, interests, and prior knowledge of students. They also learn to instruct in ways that make learning exciting and fun.

Schools that show CARE have safety nets to ensure no student falls through the cracks. They have systems for promptly identifying

"In the global economy & society of the 21st century, all children will be left behind if their education is not organized with a global context in mind."

—Goldman Sachs Foundation

"Assessment for learning, when done well, is one of the most powerful, high-leverage strategies for improving student learning that we know of. Educators collectively become more skilled and focused at assessing, disaggregating and using student achievement as a tool for ongoing improvement."

— Michael Fullan

students who are having difficulty learning key content and for responding effectively. Intervention programs are evaluated regularly to ensure that they are meeting student needs.

Truth 5: Leaders monitor progress.

In schools that show CARE, leaders monitor both student performance and teacher instructional improvement regularly. They spend significant time observing instruction. Leaders analyze data in ways that allow them to assess the impact of programs, policies, and practices — they know what progress is made and where attention is needed. Leaders also help to ensure that instructional time is used wisely and that distractions are minimized. They help maximize coordination across disciplines so that academic skills are reinforced in powerful ways.

Beyond that, leaders celebrate achievement based on data about progress towards goals — both big and small accomplishments are celebrated. They continuously remind people about the ways in which their efforts will change lives. By acknowledging progress, leaders inspire commitment, which generates more progress, which leads to greater acknowledgment of effort, and so on.

Truth 6: In schools that show CARE, the community has a common and inclusive vision of what it wants for its children.

Schools that show CARE know what they want for their children and mobilize their collective resources to realize that vision. As educators, we should work closely with other organizations and individuals concerned with the well-being of children and families. Together, we can promote more strategic and systematic approaches to improving outcomes for all students.

Since the path to supporting children — and their families — lies largely within our education system, we need to provide strong leadership to address this issue: Leadership that brings with it ability and passion for engaging various points of view, leadership that defines the agenda and the questions that need to be addressed; leadership that marshals the necessary resources to get on with meeting the mandate and makes the funding case, and most important, leadership that helps us to be explicit about what we know.

All citizens, alongside families and numerous agencies and organizations, share responsibility for preparing our nation's youth for adulthood. Deepened public engagement can harness the proven power of community involvement in education. Together, we must ensure the availability of opportunities and programs that promote the development of all children. We especially share a social responsibility to create better opportunities for the poor and to act to ensure that there are social services for children and families experiencing difficulties. Working jointly to support the development of children and youth is the most effective strategy for achieving our educational goals for them and for preventing youth problems.

Schools are — or can be — one of the main engines of social change. They can set the tone for society in ways no other institution can match. Places of education, they can also serve as vehicles for individual transformation — we must always remember that students are partners in

"The first school district, or even individual school that has the courage to accept Learning for All as its aim and takes the necessary steps to design a system to deliver that aim, will be the educational leader for the 21st century."

— Larry Lezotte, *Learning for All*

"Education is not the filling of a pail, but the lighting of a fire."

— William Butler Yeats

113

change, not merely targets of change efforts and services. Through Caring, Accepting, Respecting, and Engaging — in short, through CARE — as well as academic rigor, schools can enable people to rise above the most difficult of circumstances, including poverty, the challenges of single-parent families, and inner-city life.

American social reformer Frederick Douglass reminds us that the accomplishment of any just cause requires hard work day in and day out: "Let me offer you a word on social reform . . . those who profess freedom and depreciate agitation are men who want crops without plowing up the ground — the ocean without the mighty roar of its water, or rain without lightning and thunder. If there is no struggle, there is no progress."

In committing to the development of schools that show CARE, we have such a cause. Schools that show CARE — authentic community schools — can and *do* make a difference. By embracing Achieving, Believing, and Caring, we can create schools that CARE!

Criteria for Schools That Show CARE

Educators may use these criteria as a guide to transforming their school into one that shows CARE or as a standard against which to determine whether their school is already such a community school.

You can rate your school from 1 to 4, with 1 indicating a low rating and 4 a high rating; NA means Not Applicable.

1 2 3 4 N/A	Criteria
_____	Schools that show CARE reach out to provide parent education for families with newborns and infants; help coordinate and provide educational opportunities for three- and four-year-old children and offer full-day Kindergarten.
_____	Schools that show CARE help every child become a competent and confident reader by the end of Grade 1.
_____	Schools that show CARE implement a balanced approach in early teaching of reading and math, driven by the student's strengths and needs.
_____	Schools that show CARE encourage greater participation in art and music at all grade levels and also use this instruction to foster academic growth in other areas.
_____	Schools that show CARE initiate character education as early as Grade 2 — with reading, writing, and speaking tasks that focus on reasonable rules of behavior, taking responsibility for one's actions, and recognizing responsibility to others.
_____	Schools that show CARE have more challenging hands-on, out-of-school science and social studies problem-solving projects and make greater use of technology.
_____	Schools that show CARE and have Junior High students try to keep open until evening hours for recreation, enrichment, remedial work, hobbies, and tutoring/mentoring.
_____	Schools that show CARE make the teaching of communication (reading, writing, speaking) and problem-solving skills clear goals of every teacher and every subject matter.
_____	Schools that show CARE strive to take a more personal approach (smaller organizational units) and to communicate with every student and family regularly.

1 2 3 4 N/A	Criteria
_____	In schools that show CARE, the teaching and learning process is central. This vision embraces best practices and enables all members of the learning community to engage in challenging experiences and opportunities that will equip them to address complex problems and social issues.
_____	Schools that show CARE have academically rigorous school-to-career programs, including work experience, job shadowing, and practice in completing a job application and communicating well in a job interview.
_____	Schools that show CARE use alternatives to out-of-school suspension and design discipline to change student behavior.
_____	Schools that show CARE engage older students in helping younger ones to understand the values of honesty, dependability, respect, and kindness, as well as managing disappointment and anger.
_____	In schools that show CARE, the curriculum engages the staff and students, and prepares them for future challenges. Their vision of curriculum excellence is to provide wide educational opportunities that enable all students to reach their potential.
_____	Schools that show CARE adopt challenging curriculum and performance standards aligned with assessments and allow students to gain a deeper understanding of the core of each subject.
_____	In schools that show CARE, parents are acknowledged as the child's first teacher. This vision for excellence encourages parent and family involvement in creating a positive learning environment both at home and at school. Educators, parents, and students work as a team to support all students in reaching their full potential. When parents are actively involved, student achievement and development are enhanced and enriched.
_____	Schools that show CARE attend to the lifetime skills necessary for physical fitness and mental health through a comprehensive approach to health and wellness.
_____	In schools that show CARE, staff, students, and parents care for, respect, and trust one another. They have a common purpose and a sense of belonging, cohesiveness, and pride in the school. Morale is high, and social and academic growth are continuous.
_____	Schools that show CARE break down the barriers of the school day and year, as well as the traditional use of school buildings, and work with government, youth groups, and community groups to reach more students more effectively.
_____	Schools that show CARE work with community groups to find a way to keep school buildings open and available to the public on Saturdays, during vacations, and before and after school hours.
_____	Schools that show CARE develop unique, specialized programs of choice and allow district-wide enrolment in them.

1 2 3 4 N/A	Criteria
_____	In schools that show CARE, assessment is a balanced, seamless, and ongoing process that focuses on what students need to know and be able to do. The assessment system provides direction for continuous improvement, effective teaching and learning, and the establishment of a positive school environment.
_____	Schools that show CARE consider adding a family resource centre and school-based health clinic, where necessary and/or possible.
_____	Schools that show CARE disaggregate all school data by racial/ethnic group, gender, and parental income; they clearly identify the gaps between groups of students and take new approaches to close those gaps.
_____	Schools that show CARE engage in a data-driven plan that maximizes the contribution of each teacher and staff member in improving student achievement.
_____	Schools that show CARE support and provide professional development to all staff in the context of district-wide unifying goals and curriculum; they provide constructive feedback on how to improve instruction.
_____	Schools that show CARE have special programs or policies put in place as a result of data analysis.
_____	Schools that show CARE routinely collect achievement data by race, gender, national origin, and disability, which is analyzed with the purpose of identifying needs and successful learning strategies.
_____	In schools that show CARE, the Board of Education and administration are committed to hiring and retaining individuals with expertise in their respective roles.
_____	Schools that show CARE modify curriculum objectives and instructional strategies in light of achievement-data analysis.
_____	Schools that show CARE ensure that all school events, awards, and programs reflect the diversity of their student body.
_____	Schools that show CARE recognize the need for important events and celebrations in the school that emphasize human unity and diversity. Examples include Earth Day, World Peace Day, United Nations Day, and International Women's Day.
_____	Schools that show CARE plan events and celebrations that reflect the heritage of diverse people. Examples include Martin Luther King Day, Women's History Month, Hispanic Heritage Month, and Asian Pacific Heritage Month.
_____	Schools that show CARE ensure that pictures, decorations, and symbols in the school reflect the diversity of its population and emphasize the message of unity and diversity.

References

Adejumo, Christopher O. 2002. "Five Ways to Improve the Teaching and Understanding of Art in the Schools." *Art Education* 55 (5).

Averch, Harvey A., et al. 1972. *How Effective Is Schooling?* Santa Monica, CA: Rand Corporation.

Bafumo, Mary Ellen. 2004. "Adding the Arts." *Teaching Pre K–8* 34 (6).

Barth, Roland. 1979. "Home-Based Reinforcement of School Behavior: A Review and Analysis." *Review of Educational Research* 49:436–58.

————. 2001. *Learning by Heart*. San Francisco, CA: Jossey-Bass.

Barton, P. E. 2003. *Parsing the Achievement Gap: Baselines for Tracking Classroom Progress*. Policy Information Report. Princeton, NJ: Educational Testing Service.

Becker, H. J., and R. E. Anderson. 1998. "Validating Self-Reports of the Constructivism of Teachers' Beliefs and Practices." Paper presented at the American Educational Research Association, San Diego, CA. April.

Becker, H. J., and M. M. Riel. 1999. "Teacher Professionals, School Work Culture and the Emergence of Constructivist-Compatible Pedagogies." Paper presented to the annual meeting of the American Educational Research Association, Montreal.

Benard, B. 1995. "Fostering Resiliency in Urban Schools. In *Closing the Achievement Gap: A Vision to Guide Change in Beliefs and Practice*, ed. B. Williams. Oak Brook, IL: Research for Better Schools and North Central Regional Educational Laboratory.

Beyer, D. 1997. "School Safety and the Legal Rights of Students." *ERIC Digest*. Eugene, OR: ERIC Clearinghouse on Urban Education.

————. n.d. "School Violence and the Legal Rights of Students. http://eric-web.tc.columbia.edu/monographs/uds/uds107/school_contents.html.

Billig, S., D. Jesse, L. Calvert, and K. Kleimann. 1999. "An Evaluation of Jefferson County School District's School-to-Career Partnership Program." Denver, CO: RMC Research.

Billig, S., and J. Conrad. 1997. "An Evaluation of the New Hampshire Service-Learning and Educational Reform Project." Denver, CO: RMC Research.

Billig, S., and N. Kraft. 1998. *Linking Federal Programs and Service-Learning: A Planning, Implementation, and Evaluation Guide*. Lancaster, PA: Technomics Publishers.

Blank, M., A. Melaville, and B. Shah. 2003. *Making the Difference: Research and Practice in Community Schools*. Washington, DC: Coalition for Community Schools/Institute for Educational Leadership.

Blum, R. W., T. Beuhring, and P. M. Rinehart. 2000. "Protecting Teens: Beyond Race, Income and Family Structure." Minneapolis: University of Minnesota, Center for Adolescent Health.

Bradley, R. H., L. Whiteside-Mansell, and R. F. Corwyn. 1997a. *Early Adolescent HOME Inventory: Information on Usefulness & Validation in Four Racial/Ethnic Groups*. Paper presented at the annual meeting of the American Educational Research Association, Chicago. March.

————. 1997b. "Children in Poverty." In *Handbook of Prevention and Treatment with Children and Adolescents: Intervention in the Real World Context*, ed. T. Ammerman and M. Hersen, 13–58. New York: John Wiley and Sons.

Braeden, S., and B. Braeden. 1988. "Responding to Death and Grief in a School." *The Pointer* 32 (4): 27–31.

Brendtro, L. K., M. Brokenleg, and S. V. Bockern. 1990. *Reclaiming Youth at Risk: Our Hope for the Future*. Bloomington, IN: National Educational Service.

Briggs Myers, I. 1980. *Gifts Differing*. Palo Alto, CA: Consulting Psychologists Press.

Bradley, R. L. 2005. "K–12 Service-Learning Impacts: A Review of State-Level Studies of Service-Learning." In *Growing to Greatness 2005: The State of Service-Learning Project*, ed. J. Kielsmeier and M. Neal. Saint Paul, MN: National Youth Leadership Council.

Brodinsky, B. 1980. *Student Discipline: Problems and Solutions.* Arlington, VA: American Association of School Administrators.

Brophy, J. E. 1983. "Research on the Self-Fulfilling Prophecy and Teacher Expectations." *Journal of Educational Psychology* 75:631–61.

———. 1996. "Enhancing Students' Socialization: Key Elements." *ERIC Digest.* Eugene, OR: ERIC Clearinghouse on Educational Management.

———, and T. L. Good. 1986. "Teacher Behavior and Student Achievement. In *Handbook of Research on Teaching*, 3d ed., ed. M. C. Wittrock, 328–75. New York: Macmillan.

Bryk, A. S., and B. Schneider. 2002. *Trust in Schools: A Core Resource for Improvement.* New York: Russell Sage.

Burnett, Gary, and Walz, Garry. 1994. "Gangs in Schools." *ERIC Digest 99.* New York: ERIC Clearinghouse on Urban Education.

Catsambis, S. 1998. *Expanding Knowledge of Parental Involvement in Secondary Education: Effects on High School Academic Success.* CRESPAR Report 27. Baltimore: Johns Hopkins University. http://www .csos. jhu.edu/crespar/techReports/ Report27.pdf (accessed 25 May 2005).

Catsambis, S., and J. E. Garland. 2003. *Parental Involvement in Students' Education during Middle School and High School* (CRESPAR Report 18). Baltimore: Johns Hopkins University. http://www.csos.jhu.edu/ crespar/techReports/Report18.pdf (accessed 25 May 2005).

Catterall, J. S., R. Chapleau, and J. Iwanaga. 1999. "Involvement in the Arts and Human Development." In *Champions of Change: The Impact of the Arts on Learning*, ed. E. B. Fiske. Washington, DC: Arts Education Partnership.

Center for Mental Health in Schools. 1999. *Expanding Education Reform to Address Barriers to Learning: Restructuring Student Support Services and Enhancing School–Community Partnerships.* Los Angeles: Center for Mental Health in Schools.

———. 2000. *A Sampling of Outcome Findings from Interventions Relevant to Addressing Barriers to Learning.* Los Angeles: Center for Mental Health in Schools.

Cochran, M., and C. R. Henderson, Jr. 1986. "Family Matters: Evaluation of the Parental Empowerment Program: Summary of a Final Report to the National Institute of Education." Ithaca, NY: Cornell University Department of Human Development.

Coleman, James, et al. 1966. *Equality of Educational Opportunity.* Washington, DC: U.S. Government Printing Office.

Collins, Jim. 2001. *Good to Great: Why Some Companies Make the Leap . . . And Others Don't.* New York: Harper Business.

Collins, Randall. 1979. *The Credential Society: An Historical Sociology of Education.* New York: Academic Press.

Combs, A. W. 1982. *A Personal Approach to Teaching: Beliefs That Make a Difference.* Boston: Allyn & Bacon.

Comer, James P. 1987. "New Haven's School–Community Connection." *Educational Leadership* 44:13–16.

Comer, James P., and M. Haynes. 1991. "Parent Involvement in Schools: An Ecological Approach." *Elementary School Journal* 91:271–78.

Connell, J. P., M. A. Gambone, and T. J. Smith. 2000. "Youth Development in Community Settings: Challenges to Our Field and Our Approach." In *Youth Development Issues: Challenges and Directions*, ed. Public/Private Ventures, 281–324. Philadelphia: Public/Private Ventures.

Cornell, D. G. 1999. "What Works in Youth Violence Prevention." In *Youth Violence Prevention in Virginia: A Needs Assessment*, ed. D. Cornell, A. Loper, A. Atkinson, and P. Sheras. Virginia Department of Health.

Corter, C., and J. Pelletier. 2004. "The Rise and Stall of Parent and Community Involvement in Schools. Schools, Families, and Communities: Which Relationships Matter Most?" *Orbit* 34 (3): 7–12. http:// www. scribd.com/doc/2210749/Rise-and-Stall-of-Parent-and-Community-Involve-Carl -Corter.

Covitt, B. 2002. "Motivating Environmentally Responsible Behavior through Service-Learning." In *Service-Learning through a Multidisciplinary Lens*, vol. 2 of *Advances in Service-Learning Research*, ed. S. H. Billig and A. Furco, 177–97. Greenwich, CT: Information Age.

Dávila, A., and M. Mora. 2007. *Civic Engagement and High School Academic Progress: An Analysis Using NELS Data.* College Park, MD: The Center for Information & Research on Civic Learning & Engagement.

Dei, G. S. N. 2006. "Meeting Equity Fair and Square." Keynote address to the Leadership Conference of the Elementary Teachers' Federation of Ontario, held in Mississauga, Ontario. September 26.

De la Harpe, B., M. Kulski, and A. Radloff. 1999. "How Best to Document the Quality of Our Teaching and Our Students' Learning?" In *Teaching in the Disciplines/Learning in Context*, ed. K. Martin, N. Stanley, and N. Davison, 108–13. Proceedings of the 8th Annual Teaching Learning Forum. http://cleo.murdoch.edu.au/asu/pubs/tlf/tlf99/ dj/delaharpe.html.

Delpit, L. 1996. "The Politics of Teaching Literate Discourse." In *City Kids, City Teachers: Reports from the Front Row*, ed. W. Ayers and P. Ford. New York: New Press.

DeWit, David, Christine McKee, Jane Field, and Kim Karioja. 2003. "The Critical Role of School Culture in Student Success." December. www.voicesforchildren.ca.

Diamond. Marian. 1999. "What Are the Determinants of Children's Academic Successes and Difficulties?" Paper presented at a conference sponsored by the Harvard Children's Initiative on "Getting It Right about Children's Development: The Influences of Nature and Nurture." 5 February.

Dishion, T. J., D. Capaldi, K. M. Spracklen, and F. Li. 1995. "Peer Ecology of Male Adolescent Drug Use." *Development and Psychopathology* 7:803–24.

Dodge, D. T., and L. J. Colker. 1992. *The Creative Curriculum for Early Childhood*, 3d. ed. Washington, DC: Teaching Strategies.

Dryfoos, Joy G. 1991. "School-Based Social and Health Services for At-Risk Students." *Urban Education* (April): 118–27.

———. 1993a. "Full-Service Schools: What They Are and How to Get to Be One." NASSP *Bulletin* (December): 29–35.

———. 1993b. "Schools as Places for Health, Mental Health, and Social Services." *Teachers College Record* (Spring): 540–67.

———. 1994. *Full-Service Schools: A Revolution in Health and Social Services for Children, Youth, and Families.* San Francisco: Jossey-Bass.

———. 1995. "Full-Service Schools: Revolution or Fad? *Journal of Research on Adolescence* 5 (2): 147–72.

———. 1996. "Full-Service Schools." *Educational Leadership* (April): 18–23.

———. 1998. *Making It through Adolescence in a Risky Society: What Parents, Schools and Communities Can Do.* New York: Oxford University Press.

———. 2000. "The Mind–Body-Building Equation." *Educational Leadership* (March): 14–17.

———. 2002. "Full-Service Community Schools: Creating New Institutions." *Phi Delta Kappan* (January): 393–99.

Eadie, Doug. *Five Habits of High Impact Boards.* Lanham, Md.: ScarecrowEducation.

Eccles, J. S., and R. D. Harold. 1993. "Parent School Involvement during the Early Adolescent Years." *Teachers College Record* 94 (3): 568–87.

Edmonds, Ronald. 1979. "Effective Schools for the Urban Poor." *Educational Leadership* (October): 15–24.

Elias, Maurice J., and John F. Clabby. 1992. *Building Social Problem-Solving Skills: Guidelines from a School-Based Program.* San Francisco: Jossey-Bass.

Epstein, J. 1984. "School Policy and Parent Involvement: Research Results." *Educational Horizons* 62:70–72.

———. 1992. "School and Family Partnerships." In *Encyclopedia of Educational Research*, 6th ed., ed. M. Alkin. New York: MacMillan.

———, and S. Dauber. 1991. "School Programs and Teacher Practices of Parent Involvement in Inner-City Elementary and Middle Schools." *Elementary School Journal* 91:289–306.

Erikson, Erik H. (1985; 1963). *Childhood and Society.* New York: W.W. Norton.

Fine, C. (with L. Raack). 1994. "Overview. Professional Development: Changing Times." *Policy Briefs* (Report 4). Oak Brook, IL: North Central Regional Educational Laboratory. http://www.ncrel.org/sdrs/pbriefs/94/94–4over.htm.

Fine, Michelle. 1986. "Why Urban Adolescents Drop into and out of Public High School." *Teachers' College Record* (Spring): 393–409.

Finn, Jeremy D. 1989. "Withdrawing from School." *Review of Educational Research* 59:117, 142.

———, Susan B. Gerber, and Jayne Boyd-Zaharias. 2005. "Small Classes in the Early Grades, Academic Achievement, and Graduating from High School." *Journal of Educational Psychology* 97 (2): 214–23.

Fordham, S., and J. U. Ogbu. 1986. "Black Students' School Success: Coping with the 'Burden of Acting White.'" *Urban Review* 18:176–206.

Frankel, Charles. 1971. "Equality of Opportunity." *Ethics* 81 (3).

Fullan, Michael. 2001. *Leading in a Culture of Change.* San Francisco: Jossey-Bass.

Gasman, Marybeth. 2003. "A Renaissance on the Eastside: Motivating Inner-City Youth through Art." *Journal of Education for Students Placed at Risk* 8 (4).

Gibbs, G. 1992a. *Assessing More Students.* Oxford: Oxford Brookes University.

———. 1992b. *Improving the Quality of Student Learning.* Bristol, UK: Technical and Education Services.

Goleman, Daniel. 1998. *Working with Emotional Intelligence.* New York: Bantam.

Good, M. E. 2006. *Differentiated Instruction: Principles and Techniques for the Elementary Grades.* San Rafael, CA: Dominican University of California.

Goodenow, C., and K. E. Grady. 1993. "The Relationship of School Belonging and Friends' Values to Academic Motivation among Urban Adolescent Students." *Journal of Experimental Education* 62:60–71.

Gutman, L. M., and C. Midgley. 2000. "The Role of Protective Factors in Supporting the Academic Achievement of Poor African American Students during the Middle School Transition." *Journal of Youth and Adolescence* 29:223–48.

Harden, R. M., and J. Crosby. 2000. "AMEE Guide No. 20: The Good Teacher Is More Than a

Lecturer—the Twelve Roles of the Teacher." *Medical Teacher* 22 (4): 334–47.

Harris, P. 2002. "Learning Related Visual Problems in Baltimore City: A Long-Term Program." *Journal of Optometric Vision Development* 33:75.

Henderson, A. T., and K. L. Mapp. 2002. *A New Wave of Evidence: The Impact of School, Family, and Community Connections on Student Achievement.* Austin, TX: Southwest Educational Development Laboratory.

Henderson, A. T., and N. Berla, eds. 1994. *A New Generation of Evidence: The Family Is Critical to Student Achievement.* Washington, DC: Center for Law and Education.

Hicks, John M. 2004. "It's an Attitude." *Art Education* 57 (3).

Higgins, G. 1994. *Resilient Adults: Overcoming a Cruel Past.* San Francisco, CA: Jossey-Bass.

Hillard, A. 1991. "Do We Have the Will to Educate All Children?" *Educational Leadership* 49 (1): 31–36.

Izzo, C., R. Weissberg, W. Kasprow, and M. Fendrich. 1999. "A Longitudinal Assessment of Teacher Perceptions of Parent Involvement in Children's Education and School Performance." *American Journal of Community Psychology* 27 (6): 817–39.

Jeary, J. 2001. "Students and Teachers Develop a Resource Manual for Safe and Caring Schools." *Reclaiming Children and Youth* 9 (4): 207–9.

Jencks, Christopher, et al. 1972. *Inequality.* New York: Basic Books.

Jeynes, W. H. 2005. "A Meta-Analysis of the Relation of Parental Involvement to Urban Elementary School Student Academic Achievement." *Urban Education* (40) 3: 237–69.

Knowles, Richard T. 1986. *Human Development and Human Possibility: Erikson in the Light of Heidegger.* Lanham, Md.: University Press of America.

Kohn, Alfie. 1993. "Choices for Children: Why and How to Let Students Decide." *Phi Delta Kappan.* September.

———. 1998. *What to Look for in a Classroom.* San Francisco, CA: Jossey-Bass, 1998.

Larueau, A. 1987. "Social Class Differences in Family–School Relationships: The Importance of Cultural Capital." *Sociology of Education* 60:73–85.

Lea, S. J., D. Stephenson, and J. Troy. 2003. "Higher Education Students' Attitudes to Student Centred Learning: Beyond 'Educational Bulimia.'" *Studies in Higher Education* 28 (3): 321–34.

Lee, V. E., R. F. Dedrick, and J. B. Smith. 1991. "The Effect of Social Organization of Schools on Teachers' Efficacy and Satisfaction." *Sociology of Education* 64 (3): 190–208.

Letgers, N., and E. L. McDill. 1995. "*Rising to the Challenge: Emerging Strategies for Educating Youth at Risk.*" Urban Monograph Series. Oak Brook, IL:

North Central Regional Educational Laboratory. Repr. from Schools and Students at Risk: Context and Framework for Positive Change, ed. R. J. Rossi. New York: Teachers College Press.

Letgers, N., E. L. McDill, and J. McPartland. 1993. "Section II: Rising to the Challenge: Emerging Strategies for Educating Students at Risk." In *Educational Reforms and Students at Risk: A Review of the Current State of the Art,* 47–92. Washington, DC: U.S. Department of Education, Office of Educational Research and Improvement. October. http://www.ed.gov/pubs/EdReformStudies/ EdReforms/chap6a .html (accessed January 1994).

MacDonald, I. 1996. "Zero Tolerance: Safe and Caring Schools Project." *ATA News* 31 (8). Edmonton: Alberta Teachers' Association.

———. 1997a. "The De-meaning of Schools: Seeking a Safe and Caring Environment." Paper presented to the annual meeting of the American Educational Research Association, Chicago. March 24–28. [Similar paper presented to the annual meeting of the Canadian Association for the Study of Educational Administration, St John's, NL, June 1997.]

——— 1997b. "Violence in Schools: Multiple Realities." *Alberta Journal of Educational Research* 43 (2–3): 142–56.

———. 1998. "Navigating towards a Safe and Caring School." Paper presented at the annual general meeting of the American Educational Research Association, San Diego. April 13–17.

———. 1999. "Linking Leadership and Decision-Making to the School Violence Issue." Paper presented to the annual conference of the American Educational Research Association, Montreal. April.

MacDonald, I., and J. L. da Costa. 1996. "Reframing the Meaning of Violence: Perceptions of Alberta Junior High School Students." Paper presented to the annual meeting of the American Educational Research Association, New York. April 8–12.

Macdonnell, A. J., and W. B. W. Martin. 1996. "Student Orientations to School Rules." *Alberta Journal of Educational Research* 32 (1): 57–65.

MacDougall, J. 1993. "Violence in the Schools: Programs and Policies for Prevention." Toronto: Canadian Education Association.

Mackenzie, D. L., and C. Souryal. 1994. *Multisite Education of Shock Incarceration.* Washington, DC: National Institute of Justice.

Maslow, A. H. 1962. *Toward a Psychology of Being.* New York: Van Nostrand.

Mayerhoff, Milton. 1965. "On Caring." *International Philosophical Quarterly* 5 (3): 462–74.

McLanahan, S., and G. Sandefur. 1994. *Growing up with a Single Parent: What Hurts, What Helps.* Cambridge, MA: Harvard University Press.

McMurtry, Roy, and Alvin Curling. 2008. *Review of the Roots of Youth Violence,* Volume 2: *Executive Summary.* Toronto.

McNeely, C. A., J. M. Nonnemaker, and R. W. Blum. "Promoting Student Achievement in School: Evidence from the National Longitudinal Study of Adolescent Health." *Journal of School Health* 72 (4): 138–46.

Meier, D. 1995. *The Power of Their Ideas.* Boston, MA: Beacon Press.

Meyers, C., and T. B. Jones. 1993. *Case Studies. Promoting Active Learning — Strategies for the College Classroom.* San Francisco, CA: Jossey-Bass.

Michelli, Joseph A. 2007. *The Starbucks Experience.* New York: McGraw-Hill.

Montagu, Ashley. 1970. "A Scientist Looks at Love." *Phi Delta Kappan* 51 (9): 463–67.

Moynihan, D. P. 1965. *The Negro Family: The Case for National Action.* Washington: U.S. Department of Labor.

Muller, C. 1993. "Parent Involvement and Academic Achievement: An Analysis of Family Resources Available to the Child." In *Parents, Their Children, and Schools,* ed. B. Schneider and J. S. Coleman, 77–114. Boulder, CO: Westview.

National Association of Secondary School Principals. 1996. *Safe Schools: A Handbook for Practitioners.* Reston, VA.

National Center for Educational Statistics. 1995. "Student Strategies to Avoid Harm at School." Washington, DC. www.uncg.edu/edu/ericcass/violence/docs/harm.htm.

———.1998. Appendix A. "School Practices and Policies Related to Safety and Discipline. *Indicators of School Crime and Safety.* Washington, DC: U.S. Department of Education. http://nces.ed .gov/pubs98/safety/appendixA.html.

National Crime Prevention Council. 1995. *Clear Limits and Real Opportunities: The Keys to Preventing Youth Crime.* Ottawa.

———. 1997. *Promoting Positive Outcomes in Children Six to Twelve Years Old.* Ottawa.

———. n.d. "Bullying and Victimization. The Problems and Solutions for School-Aged Children." Ottawa.

———. n.d. "Community Alternatives for Suspended Learners in Etobicoke." www.crime-prevention .org/ncpc/council/database/practice/programs/ 12–18/031.htm

———. n.d. *Crime Prevention and Community Policing: A Vital Link.* Ottawa.

———. n.d. "Programs That Open the Doors to Youth Involvement." Ottawa. http://crime-prevention .org/ncpe/publications/ youth/mobilize/ stage_e.htm.

———. n.d. *Promoting Positive Outcomes in Youth Twelve to Eighteen Years Old.*

National Education Association. n.d. "Cultivating Safe, Helpful Climate by Establishing Strong and Responsive Adult Presence. In *Safe Climates.* http://ericcass.uncg.edu/virtuallib/violence/ docs/secure. htm.

National School Boards Association. 1993. *Violence in Schools. How America's School Boards Are Safeguarding Your Children. Best Practices.* Alexandria, VA.

Noddings, N. 1988a. "An Ethic of Caring and Its Implications for Instructional Arrangements." *American Journal of Education* (February): 215–31.

———. 1988b. "Schools Face Crisis in Caring." *Education Week* (December 7): 32.

———. 1995. "Teaching Themes of Care." *Phi Delta Kappa* (May): 675–79.

Osterman, K. F. 2000. "Students' Need for Belonging in the School Community." *Review of Educational Research* 70 (3): 323–67.

Pearson, G., J. Jennings, and J. Norcross. 1999. "A Program of Comprehensive School Based Mental Health Services in a Large Urban Public School District." In *Adolescent Psychiatry: The Annals of the American Society for Adolescent Psychiatry,* ed. Lois Flaherty, 23. Hillsdale, NJ: Analytic Press.

Phelan, P., A. L. Davidson, and H. T. Cao. 1992. "Speaking up: Students' Perspectives on School." *Phi Delta Kappan* 73 (9): 695–704.

Pinkney, A. 1987. *Black Americans.* New York: Prentice-Hall.

Pittman, K. J., and M. Cahill. 1991. *A New Vision: Promoting Youth Development.* Paper presented to the House Select Committee on Children, Youth, and Families. 30 September.

———. 1992. *Youth and Caring: The Role of Youth Programs in the Development of Caring.* Paper commissioned by the Lilly Endowment Research Grants Program on Youth and Caring and presented at the Conference on Youth and Caring. February.

Reaney, L. M., K. L. Denton, and J. West. 2002, April. *Enriching Environments: The Relationship of Home Educational Activities, Extracurricular Activities and Community Resources to Kindergartners' Cognitive Performance.* Paper presented at the annual conference of the American Educational Research Association, New Orleans, LA.

Reitzammer, Ann F. 1992. "Collaboration with Health and Social Service Professionals: Preparing Teachers for New Roles." *Journal of Teacher Education* (September–October): 290–95.

Rutter, M. 1984. "Resilient Children." *Psychology Today* (March): 57–65.

Rutter, M., B. Maughan, P. Mortimore, J. Ouston, and A. Smith. 1979. *Fifteen Thousand Hours*. Cambridge, MA: Harvard University Press.

Sanders, M. G., and J. R. Herting. 2000. "Gender and the Effects of School, Family, and Church Support on the Academic Achievement of African-American Urban Adolescents." In *Schooling Students Placed at Risk: Research, Policy, and Practice in the Education of Poor and Minority Adolescents*, ed. M. G. Sanders, 141–62. Mahwah, NJ: Lawrence Erlbaum Associates.

Schargel, F. P., T. Thacker, and J. Bell. 2007. *From At Risk to Academic Excellence: What Successful Leaders Do*. Larchmont, NY: Eye on Education.

Schmoker, M. *Results: The Key to Continuous School Improvement*, 2d ed. Alexandria, VA: ASCD (Association for Supervision and Curriculum Development).

Sexton, Porter W. 1985. "Trying to Make It Real Compared to What: Implications of High School Dropout Statistics." *Journal of Educational Equity and Leadership* 5 (2): 92–106.

Shaw, Kathleen M., and Elaine Replogle. 1996. "Challenges in Evaluating School Linked Services: Toward a More Comprehensive Evaluation Framework." *Evaluation Review* 20 (4): 424–69.

Snyder, E. E., and E. Spreitzer. 1990. "High School Athletic Participation as Related to College Attendance among Black, Hispanic, and White Males: A Research Note." *Youth and Society* 21 (3): 390–98.

Spence, Christopher. 1999. *The Skin I'm In: Racism, Sport, and Education*. Halifax: Fernwood Publishing.

Staples, R. 1988. *The Black American Family*. In *Ethnic Families in America: Patterns and Variations*, 3d ed., ed. C. Mindel et al. New York: Elsevier North Holland.

Statistics Canada. 2005. "Adult Literacy and Life Skills Survey." *The Daily* (May 11).

———. 2005. "Adult Obesity in Canada: Measured Height and Weight"; "Overweight Canadian Children and Youth." Cat. no. 82–620–MWE2005001.

Stephens, R. D. 2004. "Creating Safe Learning Environments." In *Helping Students Graduate: A Strategic Approach to Dropout Prevention*, ed. F. P. Schargel and J. Smink. Larchmont, NY: Eye on Education.

Stiggins, R. J. 1997. *Student Centred Classroom Management*, 2d ed. Upper Saddle River, NJ: Prentice-Hall.

Symons, C., B. Cinelli, T. Janes, and P. Groff. 1997. "Bridging Student Health Risks and Academic Achievement through Comprehensive School Health Programs." *Journal of School Health* 67 (6): 22–27.

Tomlinson, Carol Ann. 1998. "Differentiated Instruction." http://www. ascd.org/cms/objectlib/ ascdframeset/index.cfm?publication=http: //www.ascd.org/publications/ed_lead/199811/ darcangelo.html.

———. 1999. *The Differentiated Classroom: Responding to the Needs of All Learners*. Alexandria, VA: ASCD (Association for Supervision and Curriculum Development).

———. 2005. *How to Differentiate Instruction in Mixed-Ability Classrooms*. Upper Saddle River, NJ: Prentice-Hall.

———, and J. A. Mc Tighe. 2006. *Integrating Differentiated Instruction and Understanding by Design: Connecting Content and Kids*. Alexandria, VA: Association for Supervision and Curriculum Development.

United Nations Educational, Scientific and Cultural Organization (UNESCO). 2008. *Inclusive Education: The Way of the Future*. Geneva: UNESCO International Conference on Education, November 25–28.

Walker, H. M., G. Colvin, and E. Ramsey. 1995. "Antisocial Behavior in School: Strategies and Best Practices." *Disorders* 24:1–18.

Wallach, L. B. 1993. "Helping Children Cope with Violence." *Young Children* 48 (4): 4–11.

Wehlage, Gary G., and Robert A. Rutter. 1986. "Evaluation of Model Program for At-Risk Students." Paper presented at the annual meeting of the American Educational Research Association, San Francisco, CA.

Wehlage, Gary G., Robert A. Rutter, G. A. Smith, N. Lesko, and R. R. Fernandez. 1989. *Reducing the Risk: Schools as Communities of Support*. Philadelphia: Falmer Press.

Wenglinsky, H. 2000. *How Teaching Matters: Bringing the Classroom Back into Discussions of Teacher Quality*. Princeton, NJ: Educational Testing Service.

Werner, E., and R. Smith. 1989. *Vulnerable but Invincible: A Longitudinal Study of Resilient Children and Youth*. New York: Adams, Bannister, and Cox.

———. 1992. *Overcoming the Odds: High-Risk Children from Birth to Adulthood*. New York: Cornell University.

Xin, Ma. 2003. "Sense of Belonging to School: Can Schools Make a Difference?" *Journal of Educational Research* 96.

Yan, W., and Q. Lin. 2002. *Parent Involvement and Children's Achievement: Race and Income Differences*. Paper presented at the annual conference of American Educational Research Association, New Orleans. April.

Index

Acknowledgments

I owe debts of gratitude to many people who helped in the creation of this book.

When I began with an idea but with some hesitation about its feasibility, Mary Macchiusi of Pembroke Publishers supplied the encouragement I needed to get started. Mary had faith in my ability to write this book long before I did. Her support, advice, and friendship were essential to the book's completion.

Authoring a book takes the wisdom of a crowd. I will not try to mention everyone by name, but I acknowledge with thanks my friends and colleagues from the Hamilton-Wentworth District School Board and the Toronto District School Board who provided contributions and inspiration.

I am grateful to Jim Watt who, over the course of two years of interviews and conversations, displayed a level of self-awareness, candour, and depth of knowledge that never ceased to amaze me.

I am also grateful to my editor, Kate Revington, who read every chapter early and often and helped me rethink everything from structure to content. She guided me through the material of the book with a steady hand. She gave me valuable input and applied her keen eye and judgment to all facets of the book.

Finally, I thank my parents Syd and Enez for their unconditional support and my family, Marcia, Briana, and Jacob, for their patience, understanding, and love. With them at my side, I am the most fortunate of authors.